KOSTYA

My Story

KOSTYA TSZYU

With Malcolm Andrews

ABC
Books

Published by ABC Books for the
AUSTRALIAN BROADCASTING CORPORATION
GPO Box 9994 Sydney NSW 2001

Copyright © Top Ring Events Pty Ltd 2002

First published November 2002
Reprinted November 2002
Reprinted January 2003

National Library of Australia
Cataloguing-in-Publication entry
Tszyu, Kostya.
  Kostya : my story.

  ISBN 0 7333 1144 X.

  1. Tszyu, Kostya. 2. Boxers (Sports) - Australia -
Biography. 3. Boxers (Sports) - Soviet Union - Biography.
4. Boxing. I. Andrews, Malcolm, 1944- . II. Australian
Broadcasting Corporation. III. Title.

796.83092

Front cover photograph courtesy of Associated Press Images/Paul Connors
Back cover photograph courtesy of Associated Press Images/Lori Cain
Map produced by Lorenzo Lucia
Designed by Berney Technologies
Set in Baskerville Classico
Colour reproduction by Colorwize Studio, Adelaide
Printed and bound in Australia by Griffin Press, Adelaide

5 4 3

CONTENTS

Map of Russia — v

1 Mind Games — 1

2 The Tszyu Heritage — 5

3 Papa's Guiding Hand — 11

4 Date with Destiny — 18

5 A Mild Hiccup — 26

6 I Didn't Lose the Fight, But … — 29

7 Love is in the Air — 42

8 Goodwill to all Men — 47

9 On Top of the World — 54

10 The Three Musketeers — 65

11 Farewell to Mother Russia — 69

12 Lost in the Translation — 74

13 A New Friend Out of the Blue — 83

14 My Own Olympic Final — 87

15 Black Friday — 92

16 House Hunting — 97

17 Do and Dare — 101

18 Surprise Wedding   105

19 A Close Shave   108

20 A New Tszyu   113

21 Triumph Soured   116

22 The Black Mamba   126

23 Wet and Wild   129

24 Not Just a Palooka   136

25 Give Us Back Our Pants   142

26 Cool as a Cucumber   149

27 Vincit Qui Se Vincit   157

28 Return to the Ring   167

29 $4 Million Knockout Blow   173

30 Champion Once Again   181

31 Beware of Crocodiles   185

32 The Angel of Destruction   192

33 Little Big Man   203

34 The Winner Takes All   219

    Epilogue   233

    The Greatest   236

    Dramatis Personae   238

    My Amateur Career   244

    My Professional Career   245

    Boxing Terms   248

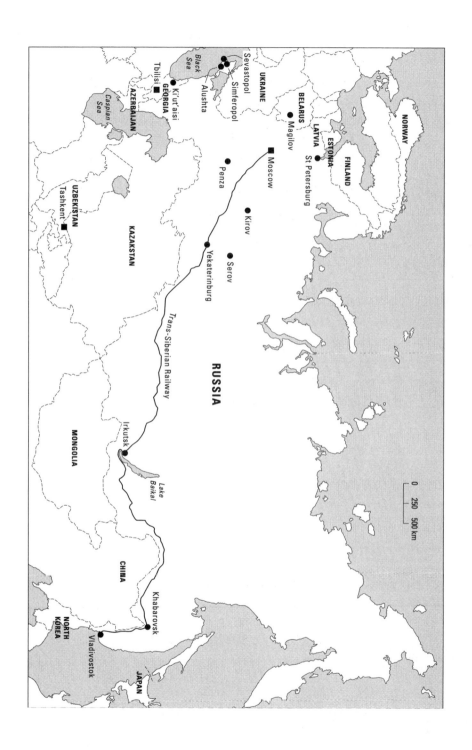

MIND GAMES

Zab Judah had a big mouth. And when he opened it, he couldn't help himself. Self-effacement wasn't a word in his vocabulary. But self-importance and self-promotion certainly were.

Zab Judah was a brash 22-year-old American boxer who, because of his fists and his mouth, became an important part of my life in 2001. He was the junior-welterweight champion of the world as recognised by the International Boxing Federation (IBF), one of three major organisations that run the sport. At the same time I was the world titleholder in the eyes of the other two groups, the World Boxing Council (WBC) and the World Boxing Association (WBA). Of course, it was (and still is) patently absurd that every weight division should have more than one champion. In the junior-welterweight at least I was determined to get rid of the anomaly by unifying the three titles. To do that I had to step into the ring with the trash-talking Zab Judah in Las Vegas on 3 November 2001.

The media loved the way he bad-mouthed opponents. Anything for a quick newspaper headline or a 10-second grab on television. The American journalists loved him.

The famous Australian Rugby League coach Jack Gibson had a few things to say about people mouthing off.

'A closed mouth gathers no foot,' was one Gibson proverb. 'Be sure the brain is engaged before putting the mouth into gear,' was another. It was obvious Zab Judah had no time for the philosophies of people like Jack Gibson.

Judah had sought to belittle my ability in the ring at every opportunity. 'Comparing Tszyu with me is like comparing a Toyota four-wheel drive with a Mercedes,' he would sneer. That brought a smile to my face because our unification bout was to be staged in Las Vegas, in the middle of the Nevada desert. And 4WDs come in quite handy in the desert.

There was his suggestion that he was going to make me look like a piece of Swiss cheese after he punched so many holes in me. Chance would be a fine thing! Anyway, years in the sport had taught me that boxing is not about words. It is about deeds in the ring. I know it's a cliché, but I had always let my fists do the talking.

Then there is the mental approach to life in the boxing ring. It is a fact of life that every one of us can be aggressive. At some stage every person in this world has the urge to fight. But not everyone can control his or her aggressive urges, harness these impulses and use them to advantage. That is the secret of a good boxer.

I always want my opponents to be aggressive. I want them to be as mad as hell, to lose their cool, maybe panic a bit. If I get them to a stage where they lose control I have them beaten.

With me, aggression comes and goes according to whether I want it to use it or not. It's like throwing a switch. One minute it is there, the next it isn't. I am in control. Preparing for a major fight one must involve oneself in mind games. You'll often see boxers lose their cool at the weigh-in before the bout. One moment all is calm, with the two opponents trying to stare each other down. The next they are trading blows, going hammer and tongs. They have both lost it.

These mind games are all about trying to make your opponent do things you want him to do, without him realising. Maybe you make him make a step towards you to shake hands, rather than you make the first move. Maybe you tell him things he doesn't expect to hear. I make sure I am always well versed on what my opponent has been doing. This goes back to my early days as an amateur, when I would write down in my diary everything I could find out about the fellow I was due to fight. I still do, only these days I read all the newspaper and magazine clippings about my opponent, watch all his television interviews on video. I get to know him almost as well as his wife or girlfriend would.

So it was with Zab Judah. I knew his partner had given birth to a baby girl a couple of months earlier. So the first thing I said to him when we met at the weigh-in 24 hours before the fight was, 'How's your daughter getting on?' He had approached me ferociously, almost ready to start throwing punches. But my question threw him. I could almost see his brain ticking over, 'Why is he asking me this question?' 'Ah, um, okay,' he mumbled. Then I put my arm around his shoulders and whispered in his ear. 'Having children is a great experience isn't it? Better even than winning a world title?' I gave a knowing nod of the head, smiling with my face only centimetres from his. He did not know what to say. He was grasping for words that never came. His reactions were lost in a dry throat that refused to allow any sounds through. I had broken his mental preparation. I had him on the back foot even before we had traded the first blows.

It didn't end there. Two days before the fight we had each been given two hours to train in the ring in which the bout would be fought. His session was scheduled to be first at around 11am. Mine would follow immediately after his. Zab and his team intentionally delayed his time in the ring so that when we arrived we couldn't start our session. This was a tactic that was designed to upset me. On the contrary. I turned the situation around to suit myself. I made sure we sent officials into his session every few minutes with demands that he leave. When he didn't, my team sent for the police to have him evicted. In the meantime, I just sat in a nearby lounge and quietly meditated. I was completely relaxed. Eventually he tired of the game and left. His tactics had backfired on him. His training session had been a disaster. I was able to have my scheduled two hours, albeit a little late, but without any inter-ruptions. And it was probably the most fruitful training session I had had since arriving in the United States. I knew then that there was no way I would lose the fight with Zab Judah!

THE TSZYU HERITAGE

The Tszyu story begins in Korea a few hundred years ago. Just how many hundred, I am not sure.

I am proud of my Korean heritage — sketchy as the details are about it. One of the real regrets of my life is that I seem destined never to find out those details of my ancestry.

My great-grandfather migrated from Korea to Russia around the start of the 20th century. None of my family knows why. My grandfather probably could have explained, but he was tight-lipped about the family's past. Like all those who lived through the horrors of the Stalin era in the Soviet Union he had an inherent distrust of people questioning him about his past. Who could blame him?

But my great-grandfather would have been like many of his countrymen, who left Korea in the late 19th and early 20th century seeking a better life for their families. Koreans have a noble tradition, the Kingdom of Choson (or Land of the Morning Calm) stretching back to 2333BC. Because of its strategic location, many nearby countries cast envious eyes in its direction. In the late 1800s, Russia, China and Japan all manoeuvred politically and economically with the aim of annexing Korea and adding it to their respective empires. In 1910 Japan moved in militarily and imposed a harsh regime that was to last until the empire's defeat by the Allies in World War II.

Maybe my great-grandfather preferred the rule of the Russians and moved with his family to Vladivostok. Maybe they were moved forcibly. I can only begin to imagine what made him leave his homeland. Going on the background of my immediate family, I believe my great-grandfather was a caring man who spoke out against any injustices and probably did not behave the way the authoritarian Japanese expected. Ironically, he would have moved from one authoritarian state to another.

Of course, under the totalitarian regime of the Soviet Communist dictator Josef Stalin, such non-conformity would have been viewed with intense distaste by the authorities. My great-grandfather's family was broken up and forcibly scattered around the Soviet Union in 1937. This is of no surprise. What is surprising is that they survived at all. History shows how in that year Stalin began the so-called 'Great Purges'. Academics have called 1937 Stalin's Year of Terror. There are various estimates of the number of citizens slaughtered at Stalin's behest. One million? Ten? Another nine million arrested? The 1937 census apparently showed a figure of 30 million Soviet citizens missing. Stalin was not amused and those responsible for the census disappeared. It is suggested that in a single year (1937) six times more people were shot than the total number killed in all the other years of the Soviet Union put together. Stalin killed off most of his senior military commanders and political opponents.

The Tszyu family was 'lucky' in that its members were scattered around the Soviet Union, relocated in various cities rather than being shot or sent to the gulags (concentration camps). My grandfather, Timophey Tszyu, ended up in Serov. I have since discovered another branch of the family in Tashkent. And, for all I know, other members of the family could have been sent to various far-flung reaches of the Soviet Union. As records were destroyed by the authorities to hide the extent of Stalin's terror campaign, I will never be able to track them down, so we'll never know.

My own story begins on Friday, 19 September 1969, when I was born in the Soviet industrial city of Serov in the Bogslovsk district on the southern slopes of the Urals, the massive mountain range that cuts a swathe through the wastelands of Siberia.

I was the first child of Boris and Valentina Tszyu. Papa was a fitter and turner at the local steelworks, and Mama, whose family originally came from Kirov, was a nurse in the local hospital.

I very nearly didn't make it into this world. Mama had a long and painful labour, about 48 hours, and when I first made my appearance the medical staff thought I was stillborn. There was none of the usual throaty yelling of a newborn baby and the doctors had to work feverishly for several minutes to get my heart beating. When they did there was no looking back.

Was it an omen? A tough start, readying me for the tough fight in later life to prove myself the best in the world?

Like all industrial cities around the world, Serov is hardly picture postcard material. It is (and has been for more than a century) grim and foreboding. The city itself had its beginnings in May 1894, when a new steel mill was built amid heavy forest on the bank of the River Kakva. The mill and the township that sprang up around it were originally named Nadezhdinsk after the rich landowner who had control of vast tracts of land in the district. In January 1896 the first steel rolled off the mills, most of it to be used in the construction of the Trans-Siberian Railway, which when finished in

1916 linked Moscow to the eastern seaport of Vladivostok. One of the key stations of the 9300 kilometre railroad was Ekaterinburg (later Sverdlovsk and now Yekaterinburg), a city some 400 kilometres to the south of Serov. Today Serov is home to around 1.6 million people. Many of them were forcibly settled there in the years leading up to World War II as the leadership in Moscow realised that war was imminent and knew Serov would be the most important supplier of steel for the war effort.

In 1939, the Soviet authorities changed the name of my hometown as the Communist leadership was unimpressed by the fact that such a key city should commemorate a capitalist. They decided, instead, to honour one of the Soviet Union's greatest biplane fighter pilots and a native of the North Urals, Lieutenant General Anatoly Konstantinovich Serov. He had made a name for himself fighting on the side of the republicans against the forces of General Franco in the Spanish Civil War.

Lieutenant General Anatoly Konstantinovich Serov, Hero of the Soviet Union

Anatoly Serov was born in 1910 in Vorontsovka (later Kalinino) in the North Urals. He joined the Red Army in 1929 and graduated from air college two years later, the same year that he joined the Bolshevik (Communist) Party. From then until 1937 he worked as a test pilot.

That same year he went to Spain as one of the many Soviet pilots who fought for the republicans in the Spanish Civil War. He flew as a fighter pilot under the Spanish alias of Rodriguez Mateu. He was involved in many of the most celebrated air battles during the conflict. At one stage his squadron played a crucial role in the air defences of Madrid. He and another Soviet air ace, Mikhail Yakushin, organised a night-fighter group to combat bombing raids after dark by the forces of General Franco. The republican government rewarded both Serov and Yakushin with gold watches and personal cars for their efforts.

Serov later flew sorties over Barcelona, Valencia and Zaragoza. He claimed eight biplane 'kills' in 48 aerial dogfights during his one year in Spain. He shared the credit with another pilot for shooting down another eight aircraft.

Back in the Soviet Union Serov was promoted to the rank of Lieutenant General just before he was killed in an aircraft crash on 11 May 1939. He was buried in Moscow's Red Square, just outside the walls of the Kremlin.

When I was 18 months old I was sent to kindergarten. Everyone did in Russia. Our parents had to work. Papa worked in the steel works from 7am to 4pm every day. Mama, a nurse, worked weird 12-hour shifts, so I would often sleep overnight at kindergarten.

I started school at six. I was the smallest boy in the class and, I think, the cheekiest. I must have had some leadership qualities for even though I was so small the other boys followed me. I couldn't sit down in the one place and I used to get into trouble with the teachers because I never seemed to be listening to them. But I had an ability to listen to one person and talk to someone else on another subject at the same time. I could listen and talk and think — all at once. Today I would probably be described as hyperactive. I was probably a bit of a pain-in-the-neck as I would regularly interrupt the teachers, and never let any of the other kids answer the questions. I was bright and knew the answers so I remember thinking, 'Why shouldn't I answer all the questions'.

My family and I lived in a small apartment in Lobva, a suburb of Serov. It was Flat 64, No. 8 Korolenko House, part of a housing estate, in a two-storey house divided into four apartments. Two families lived in each apartment. The other family was better off than we were as they had two bedrooms. We had just a single bedroom about four metres by four metres. That room held all our worldly goods. Mama and Papa had a bed. My younger sister Olga had a bed and I slept on the floor. There was a table, a refrigerator and a wardrobe. I would play under the table.

We shared the kitchen with the other family. We had two hotplates on the stove each and whoever was in first for dinner got to use the oven. There were two kitchen tables — one for us and one for them. There was only one bathroom and toilet. In the morning there would always be fights with the other family about who used it. It was virtually impossible to clean yourself properly. There was only hot water if you burned a wood fire under the boiler and the local council would turn off the water overnight. There was always a lot of conflict with the neighbours. They weren't what you would call friendly.

There was a local bathhouse nearby where we would go once or twice a week. Here, there was a huge sauna and bath for each sex and the bathhouse would hold about 100 people at a time. You would wash yourself, sit in the steam and scrape the dust and dirt off your skin. At busy times you would have to wait in a queue for your turn in the community bath. There were two or three showers but they were more expensive. And then there were a couple of single baths. They were the most expensive of all. Sheer luxury.

Papa had been on a waiting list for an apartment of his own for 20 years. There were about 400 families in front of him. But it took so long for the waiting list to get shorter because people were always jumping the queue. Later in life when I became famous I was to gain first-hand knowledge of how to move to the front of the queue in Russia. Eventually all the waiting paid off for Papa and, when I was 13, we were allocated our new three-bedroom apartment. It was like winning the lottery. It was a modest dwelling — but to us it was like Buckingham Palace. No more would we have to fight for the bathroom or the kitchen. No more would we have to cram all our belongings into one tiny room. We now had our very own home.

PAPA'S GUIDING HAND

Directly after God in heaven comes Papa.
— Mozart

So often parents get criticised for pushing their children in sport. The critics claim that kids are mentally damaged by overbearing parents demanding that their sons or daughters excel on the sporting field no matter what the cost. But among the great sportsmen and women over the years there are so many examples of the guiding hand of a parent — usually a father. In tennis, Jennifer Capriati was steered back from a broken life by her father to become the best in the world; and the Williams sisters, Venus and Serena, whose father not only coached them but prepared them for life outside tennis. Golfing great Tiger Woods has been supported by his dad. And what about all those hundreds of Australian swimmers whose parents have risen at the crack of dawn every day to drive them to the pools for their training? Who is most deserving of the subsequent Olympic gold medals — the swimmers or their parents?

In my case Papa was an incredible influence. When I was a small boy he pushed me hard, he always wanted me to be a winner in everything I did. He had been a fine sportsman when he was younger, in athletics, hockey and especially wrestling. Winning meant everything to him, and he wanted me to be the same. He taught me being a 'real man' was the only way to go through life. In every discipline I attempted I had to be the best. It was such that I would break down and cry if I lost.

Looking back, I realise my Papa may have pushed me too hard at times, but in the long run all this training from such a young age has helped me greatly, and prepared me for a tough career.

It was Papa's decision that I should become a boxer. It certainly wasn't mine.

I can remember when I was about six or seven years old I got in a fight with a kid in the street. It started out as a bit of a push and a shove and then I hit this other kid and knocked him out cold. It gave me an awful fright.

My father reckoned I should go to a gym to be taught properly. I was seven when I first went to the gym, but I was a bit too young and I quit after one training session. At the age of nine I went back to the gym and took up boxing regularly. I was still very young, as most boys didn't start until they were at least 12, so at first the going was very tough. I was constantly sparring with boys older and bigger than I was. At about 10 or 11 years of age I had my first proper fight in the ring. It was against a boy from another gym in Serov. It was a case of moving up to him — boom, boom, boom — and they stopped the fight. I had won my first bout.

The second fight I lost and I was really upset by the loss, but I had my revenge. Later on I had a chance to fight this guy again on two occasions and beat him both times.

Before the new season, I heard that Vladimir Chernya, the trainer of my first couple of opponents, was looking for me as he knew that my trainer had left the gym. He asked me if I wanted to join his team across the other side of Serov? Papa was keen for me to take him up on his offer, even though it meant a lot of travel, so I linked up with Chernya in a partnership that was to last throughout my amateur career.

I would go to the gym after school, a 20-minute journey in a crowded bus. It wasn't like a bus trip in, say, Sydney or New York. The passengers would be packed in like sardines in antiquated vehicles. Often I would be holding on outside the door as the bus made its way across the city. But despite these travelling arrangements I can boast that I never once missed a training session.

It was all part of the discipline instilled in me by Chernya. He had strict rules, and you disobeyed them at your peril. If you turned up with your nails too long — you were out of the training session. If you turned up with hair that was too long — you were out of the training session. Being late was unacceptable (unless you had an excuse that you were kept at school or were ill in bed). If you were late twice you were thrown out of the team. Your boxing career was over.

I have carried this self-discipline with me into adulthood. I can't stand people who are always late for appointments. Okay, sometimes there is an acceptable reason for being late. Being caught in traffic isn't one. If there is any chance of there being heavy traffic, you should leave earlier. It is better to be early for an appointment than late. I suppose my attitude has softened a bit since I moved to Australia. The casual Aussie lifestyle encourages a bit of give and take by all of us.

Chernya may have had his hard-and-fast rules, but he was still very good when it came to handling kids. He wasn't too much older than the fellows he was training, and was about 16 years older than me. He became something between a second father and an elder brother to me. He placed a lot of emphasis on the teaching of good boxing techniques and stressed how it was important that we knew how to punch properly and to defend ourselves against a whole variety of punches. He had certain ideas that later in life I realised weren't quite right (and we had arguments about it), but in general he gave me a completely rounded boxing education.

He was always experimenting with ideas — some of which seemed quite outrageous. Diet, training, the way we would sleep — he would pursue all sorts of variations and I was usually the guinea pig. He would have all the members of his boxing team running barefoot in the snow. He started us off with a five-minute run in the snow. It was painful, very painful. Eventually he had us running for 15 minutes. When we finished we couldn't feel our frozen feet. This was a way of teaching us to overcome pain by using our powers of concentration. Then, when a time came in the ring when we were hurting, we would know how to shut out thoughts of that pain. At least, that was his theory.

Chernya would also push you to breaking point, and when he didn't I would push myself. I remember early in my career pushing so hard at training that I physically vomited in the ring. I just wiped away the vomit and continued until I vomited a second time. The idea was similar to that of running barefoot in the snow.

I vividly remember another of Chernya's experiments. I was 14 or 15 years old at the time. It was on the eve of the final of some relatively minor competition. He changed my whole lifestyle pattern. At 11pm he had me spend time in the sauna, then we ate a light meal, but he refused to let me go to bed. We just fooled around for several hours. At 8am he eventually said, 'Okay, go and have some sleep.' I couldn't believe it. I was due to fight in the final in three hours time. 'I'll let you have an hour's sleep and then wake you up.' When he came to wake me up, I protested vehemently. I was exhausted. I wanted to go back to sleep. When I explained this, all he would say was 'Good!' As it turned out I fought one of the best fights of my career that day. Afterwards he explained: 'This tournament was not important. You were always going to win it and win it well. Some time in the future you will have a difficult night when you can't sleep. Maybe because of jet lag. Maybe because you're not well. When this happens in the future you will be able to look back to this day and know that despite being deprived of sleep you can go out and fight, and fight with confidence. It is all a case of self-belief, of your subconscious knowing you can do it.'

Be smart, Kostya. You're not as strong as these older fighters, so use your brain. Remember, Kostya, brain always beats brawn.
— *coach Vladimir Chernya*

I started regular fighting in tournaments in 1980 at the age of 10. Within the next four years or so I had fought about 100 fights. My first success came in a local competition at Serov in 1982. There were about 13 or 14 boys in my weight division and I won two or three fights to take the gold medal. By the time I quit in 1991 to pursue a professional career I had fought in 270 bouts and had lost just 11.

When it came to trying for national selection, you always started in your hometown. If I won at Serov it was then off to the semi-regional tournament for another four fights before qualifying for the regional tournament in Sverdlovsk. Another four fights and you were through to the Russian Championship and finally onto the Soviet titles.

The year of 1985 was my busiest so far — especially the first six months during which I fought 28 bouts. In the Soviet Youth Games I was disappointed to lose my only fight. But that year I finally made a name for myself by winning a Russian title. I was just 15, but beat a 32-year-old in the final. Vladimir had begun putting me in against senior fighters because I had no decent local opposition against kids of my own age. He told me something I have never forgotten: 'Be smart, Kostya. You're not as strong as these older fighters, so use your brain. Remember, Kostya, brain always beats brawn.'

I lost in my first bout of the Soviet Championship that year but it did not matter. The national head trainer thought I showed a lot of promise and invited me to my first national training camp and a tournament, both at Tbilisi, the capital of the Republic of Georgia. A city of around 1.2 million people, Tbilisi is famous for its sulphur spas. Indeed, its very name comes from the Georgian word *tbili* meaning warm. There is a story how the legendary Tsar Vahtang was hunting in the area where he hoped to build his new capital. He was using a falcon to catch smaller birds. The falcon dropped one of the birds, which was later found in a hot stream, cooked by the near boiling water and ready to eat. The tsar was so impressed that he built Tbilisi on the site of where the bird was found. Or so the story goes! Nevertheless, Tbilisi plays an important part in my life as the site of the first real stepping stone to success in my boxing career.

It was a great honour to be invited to train with the national team. I arrived with Chernya and we were met in the lobby by the head trainer. He immediately turned on Chernya. 'Why are you here?' he snapped. 'You weren't invited!' Chernya was stunned and left immediately as I was taken to my room. Later the head trainer came up to me, saying, 'We've found a room for your trainer. Where is he?' I explained how he had left to go back to Serov. The head trainer just shook his head and explained, 'He didn't have to leave. I was just angry that he didn't check with me before coming.'

It was a difficult first few days for me. I knew no one and was angry that Chernya had left so hurriedly and not stood up to the head coach. That camp was the start of us moving away from each other. Chernya would always remain my coach until I eventually left Russia, but a small, if almost imperceptible, rift had begun to appear.

Although I lost in the first round of the Tbilisi tournament, my boxing career was well and truly on track. In September 1985 I journeyed outside the Soviet Union for the first time, to Czechoslovakia for an international tournament. I won my first bout against a Polish fighter, but then lost to a Bulgarian. It was no disgrace to lose as I was just 15 and the Bulgarian was a seasoned 27-year-old boxer. As far as I was concerned, the world was now my oyster.

There were still the occasional setbacks. At the start of 1986 I was told to train for a tournament in the Indonesian capital of Jakarta. I was really excited. Indonesia was somewhere I had only read about in school geography textbooks. It seemed so far away, halfway across the world. But I must have somehow upset one of the team officials because the trip never eventuated. I was devastated.

This sort of thing happened regularly in Soviet sporting teams. The head trainer had a lot of clout. I remember in the junior-middleweight (71 kilograms) division there was a sensational Armenian boxer who won the Soviet titles in both 1986 and 1987, but he never went to either the European or World Championships. Someone didn't like him. Of course, there would always be a logical explanation. The head trainer or team manager would blame it on poor sparring, or lack of fitness, or breaking team regulations like being late to bed. They always had an excuse.

The pool of boxing talent was so large that you could never rest on your laurels. There were so many fine boxers in the Soviet Union the trainers could pick and choose. Even if you were the Soviet champion you would never know until the day of selection whether or not you would be in the team. Even if you did make the team you were always just one bout away from disaster. A bad loss and it was back to square one with no earnings or a position on the team. It could be disastrous. You have to understand that as a 15-year-old boxer in the Soviet team I was earning more than my Papa did in the Serov factory where he worked.

DATE WITH DESTINY

4

This is the day I decide my own destiny. If I win today a great future is assured. The teenage scrawl in my diary said it all. The date was Monday, 10 March 1986. My first real opportunity of winning a Soviet Championship. I had been knocked out of the national titles the previous year, losing my first bout on points. But back then I was very raw and lacking in boxing expertise. The intervening 12 months had been a real learning experience for me. This time there was no thought of defeat. I was mentally prepared for ultimate victory. My destiny lay in my own two fists.

I had arrived unheralded three days earlier in the Georgian city of K'ut'aisi, about 85 kilometres east of the Black Sea. It's an historic city and, at around 3500 years old, one of the most ancient in the world. In Greek mythology it was the site of Colchis, from where Jason and the Argonauts sailed in search of the legendary Golden Fleece. The city features some wonderful old buildings and is overlooked by a magnificent extinct volcano, Mount Sataplia, but like the other boxers, I had no time for sightseeing on this trip. I was in search of my own personal Golden Fleece.

I had missed the selection trials because I had been away in training camp with the Soviet national squad. I eventually gained entry to the championships as a wildcard because of my status in the squad. But when I'd left home I didn't know for sure whether that would happen. As I explained previously, the Soviet boxing officials were a law unto themselves. And, even though you may be in the national squad, they could decide at a moment's notice whether or not you could take part in any championship. It was only when I arrived in K'ut'aisi that I knew for certain I would be taking part. When I got the green light, I felt confident, thanks to the fact that I had outclassed in sparring sessions in the gym all those who had won their way through from my area's trials.

From a couple of thousand boxers in my division who tried for selection around the various republics of the Soviet Union there were now just 23 remaining. Several would have an extra fight. My first stroke of luck occurred when it came to the ballot and I was one of those who automatically made the second round.

It wasn't going to be an easy championship baptism for me, a 16-year-old novice taking on the cream of boxers from all over the Soviet Union. Many of them had been fighting competitively for several years and had scores of fights under their belt. My regular trainer Vladimir Chernya was back in Serov. I was just a kid and I felt very much alone.

The hotel accommodation didn't help. I arrived at 8.30am on Friday and they put me in a room on the seventh floor with two other boxers. Only when looking back at my diary 15 years later did I realise that one of them, Ahmed Kotiev, went on to become WBO professional world champion in the welterweight division in 1998.

To my amazement, I found there was no hot water in the hotel. How naïve of me to assume there would be hot water. I now know it was not unusual for the hot water systems to fail in Soviet hotels. K'ut'aisi was in one of the 'warmer' areas of the southern Soviet Union. But in March the city was still wrapped in the frosty grip of winter. It was to be several days before I summoned up the courage to wash myself in the icy water that bubbled out of the tap.

I was buoyed by the results of the first round of fights, when one of the favourites for the title was beaten and would not be there come medal time. My first opponent was a boxer from Penza, an industrial city about 600 kilometres south-east of Moscow, best known as the home of one of Russia's greatest poets, Mikhail Lermantov. I don't even remember my opponent's name. But my diary recalls the preparation I made for the fight.

It was a routine I have followed over all the years of my boxing career. Step One: Find out all I can about my opponent. Step Two: Write it all down. Step Three: Read it over and over again until I am sure I know him. Don't leave anything to chance. I discovered all I could about this fellow from Penza. He was taller than me, by about a head. He was very strong, very aggressive and worked well when he got in close. We'd been in the same Soviet team training camp, but we had never sparred together. I couldn't recall having even watched him spar. I found out he could punch hard. But if he had a weakness it was that he sometimes lost his balance and rhythm when he was hit hard. I would have to work on this weakness.

I wrote down my plan for the fight in my diary. Round One I would put in single punches to the body and head. I wouldn't try to force anything. And I would try to work on counter-punching in defence. In Round Two, I would go all out in attack. Round Three would be a contrast. I would start out fighting from a distance. Then suddenly I would change tactics and come in hard in wholehearted attack.

I was given little chance to settle into a routine out of the ring as officials kept switching my room. For the second night I was moved to a room on the hotel's third floor. The next night it was back to another different room on the seventh. Unfamiliar room mates every time. But I remained focused. Nothing was going to take my mind off the task that lay ahead.

The fight itself was a complete turnaround. In the third second of the first round, all my well-laid plans went out the window. My opponent had retreated into a defensive mode. It was so difficult. Neither of us really wanted to attack. We were searching out each other. The second round was no different. In the third round, I managed to force him to come to me and brought my good counter-punching into play. As he was trying to fathom out my style I went all out in attack. Attack, attack, attack! It paid off. I received the unanimous vote of the three judges. The die had been cast. I was now in control of my destiny!

There was little time to recover. My quarter-final would be fought the following day. Again, as was my custom, I made a written assessment in my diary of how I thought the previous bout had gone. I was happy with my victory over the fellow from Penza, but felt I had fought a lazy fight. That could prove my downfall against a better fighter. In future I must start my fights faster.

My quarter-final opponent was a fellow called Bounin from Tashkent, the capital of Uzbekistan, one of the republics just north of Afghanistan. I was out of bed at 6.40am and had a light 30-minute workout in the gym to loosen my muscles after the previous day's fight. I wasn't fighting until 6pm, so I had time to think about Bounin. He was very tall and extremely strong. He was a southpaw – which in boxing means he led with his right hand which he used very effectively. He had a very sharp, very speedy, left hand. I made a note to keep a close eye out for it. Bounin also liked to attack his opponents' ribs. I planned to work on counter-punching in the first round, and to go on all-out attack in the remaining two rounds.

This fight was going to be one of the hardest fights of my career as it took on added significance for me. If I won it I would achieve the status of Master of Sport in the Soviet Union. It was a great honour and one which every Soviet athlete, no matter what his or her sport, strived for. It did not often come to a 16-year-old like me. I wrote in my diary: 'I must not disappoint my [Serov] team. I must not disappoint my trainer. I must not disappoint myself.'

I lost the first round. The second was close, it could have gone either way. I made my move in the third. I walked up to Bounin. I was aggressive. I was intense. I was on fire. It was a case of hitting, hitting, hitting and more hitting. He had no answer. It was a unanimous points victory on the cards of the three judges. I was as proud as a peacock. Of the 34 in the team from my district only 12 had reached the semi-finals. And I was one of the 12.

But the win had come at a heavy cost. The fight had taken its toll. My left hand had been terribly injured. It was aching so much I couldn't even squeeze it. My lips were cut and bleeding. I was nursing what you would call a shiner, my left eye was badly bruised. I looked a real mess but I couldn't have cared less. I had won my way through to the semi-finals. There is an old Russian saying, roughly translated it says, 'it will be all fixed by the wedding'. Something like the English expression 'it will be right on the night'. In my diary, I wrote down the old saying and was confident that this would come true.

My semi-final was against a guy called Bougin. I can't remember what part of the Soviet Union he came from. He was very similar to my previous opponent, but stronger. I felt weak and sore before the bout, but my determination to do well overcame that setback. I had planned to attack from the start, but I couldn't get into my rhythm in the first round. In the final two rounds my timing was there and I regularly found openings in his defence to set up another victory.

That night I became worried. I couldn't relax properly, managing only about three hours of fitful sleep. My throat was beginning to ache and I was sweating even though the weather was quite cold. The signs were ominous. I had caught some sort of virus.

The following day was another rest day, although I wished we could have fought the final there and then to get it over and done with. I actually had my first real wash since arriving in K'ut'aisi. It didn't matter that the water was freezing, it helped refresh me. I was sick, running a temperature and coughing. The worst headache imaginable was pounding my brain. Feeling like I did, I couldn't see myself fighting in the final. But I managed to jot down the usual summary about my opponent, a guy from Armenia, the republic that bordered Turkey and Iran. 'Very smart. Good left hand. Very busy fighter. Great in close. Has a dangerous defensive punch that he executes with lightning speed and great timing.' Then I wrote something quite out of character: 'I give myself little chance of winning.' I was so sick I thought the worst.

But the human spirit knows no bounds. On the day of the final I dug deep into my inner self and found something extra. I gave everything I had and came out on top. It was a case again of hit, hit, hit ... non-stop hitting. It all paid off. I won the gold medal. I was junior amateur champion of the Soviet Union — an honour never before achieved by anyone in my hometown. I couldn't believe it. I was over the moon with the excitement of it all.

It seemed that winning was the easy part. I faced a long journey home ... a journey of more than 3000 kilometres to get home. First there was a four-hour bus trip to the Georgian capital of Tbilisi, then a three-hour plane flight to Sverdlovsk and then a 10-hour overnight train trip to Serov. The train pulled into Serov at around 5am. It was too early for the buses to be running, so I trudged the half-hour or so to Lobva on foot, weighed down by my two suitcases, one of which contained my own personal 'Golden Fleece'. The gold medal that proclaimed me as Soviet champion.

I must have looked a sight as I walked into the family apartment. I was dog-tired, bruised, battered, sweating and coughing. My parents were unaware of my victory, and they must have thought the worst as I walked down the corridor. Papa was about to leave for work and hurriedly asked how I had gone. I said nothing, reached into the suitcase and pulled out the gold medal. I'll never forget the look of astonishment on his face when he laid eyes on it. He started yelling and jumping up and down on the spot.

Eventually he calmed down and raced off to work, with a real spring in his steps, but when he told everyone what I had done, his boss immediately gave him the rest of the day off and sent him home to celebrate. 'You must be with Kostya,' he told Papa. 'No one from around here has ever achieved such a victory. You must celebrate together.'

Chernya knew I was due home and came around to see how I had gone. He, too, was ecstatic. When my father arrived home, he broke open a bottle of vodka and he and Chernya began celebrating. All day they celebrated before Chernya stumbled off on his walk home. He had no sooner got to the corner of the street than a police car pulled up alongside him and he was told to get in. The normal practice with people caught drunk in public was that the police would take them back to the cells to dry out overnight. Then their bosses would be notified and an adverse report would be added to their work record. Chernya feared the worst. But to his surprise, the next moment the police car had pulled up outside his apartment.

'We wanted to make sure you made it home safely,' said the policeman. 'Your boy has brought great honour to our town.' And with that the police car drove off.

The next day, it was back to school for one of my periodic visits. This time I had every reason to thumb my nose at a few of the teachers, who had frowned on my rebellious behaviour in the past, angry at my refusal to conform like the good little Soviet children they were trying to cultivate. Indeed, I think a couple of them had been secretly hoping I would fail in my boxing career and would be forced back into the system that demanded conformity from everyone. The disappointment showed on these teachers' faces. My other teachers were like the rest of the school, like the rest of the people of Serov, and were excited by the fame I had brought to the town.

The following month I won a silver medal at an international tournament at Schwerin in East Germany, beaten by a local boxer whose name I can't remember. Then it was off to a training camp in Cuba and back to another camp in Alushta on the Black Sea. In early August there were the 1986 Drugba (Friendship) Games in Hungary. The first Friendship Games had been held in Moscow, after the countries from the Soviet bloc (including Cuba) had boycotted the 1984 Los Angeles Olympics. But this time they were restricted to juniors. I won a bronze medal.

5
A MILD HICCUP

It was about this time that my career was almost derailed. The
constant grind of training had begun to take its toll. Despite the
success in the Soviet Championships I was tempted to throw it all
in. I should have been excited about the opportunities that awaited
me. Instead I was tired and listless. After a couple of months I got
to a stage that I couldn't care less about anything in life.

Chernya was not impressed. Perhaps he realised that I had the
potential to be world or Olympic champion and, as such, he would
be able to bask in the kudos from my success. If I quit now all his
work would have been in vain. Or maybe he was genuinely worried
I was not going to fulfil my destiny and would regret it later in life.

He took me to a training camp near Serov. I suppose the nearest
thing you would have in the West was a Boy Scouts camp. But it
was more than that. This camp was almost self-sufficient, even
growing its own food. Vladimir put me in charge of a handful of

baby chickens. My task was to look after these chicks, feed them, make sure they didn't stray or come to any harm. As the days passed I became like a mother to them. They would come running, chirping away merrily every time I appeared on the scene. They knew that I was going to feed them. I even had names for each of them. This went on for about two weeks, and then one morning Chernya came to me, put a butcher's knife in my hand and said, 'Now you will kill the chicks.'

I spluttered, 'But why? But how?'

The reply was blunt, 'I haven't the slightest idea. Do it however you like. I'm going. And, by the way, we're having them for dinner.' I eventually slit the chicks' throats. Talk about stress! People ask me what Chernya had in mind when setting me this grotesque task. I really don't know. I don't think it was to give me a killer instinct. I think he meant to show that training, which I thought was hard, was quite easy when compared with killing animals that I had nurtured. All I know was that the next day I was back in the gym training harder than I had ever done in the past.

I don't think Chernya had ever set such a test for other fighters he had trained. I look back and I'm convinced this was just another of his training and psychology experiments. If it worked for Kostya Tszyu he could always use the same methods with other fighters who came after me. Whatever his intentions, the date of the killing of the chickens is firmly etched in my mind — 17 August 1986.

A week later I journeyed to Magilov in Belarus for a camp before fine-tuning my training in Moscow in preparation for the European Junior Championships. They were held at Brondby, in the Danish capital of Copenhagen. Brondby is best known for its famous soccer team that over the years has had memorable confrontations with sides such as Manchester United and Real Madrid. At the championships I comfortably cruised through all four of my bouts (against a Spaniard, an Italian, a Romanian and a Frenchman) to win the first major international title of my career. Each of the bouts was a unanimous points decision by the five judges. There was no looking back. I was well and truly on my way. I finished the year by winning another international tournament at Tbilisi.

In January 1987, I finally made it to Indonesia, winning a tournament in Jakarta. It was then on to Irkutsk to defend my Soviet crown. Irkutsk is a city of about 750,000 people about halfway along the Trans-Siberian Railway, 70 kilometres from the massive Lake Baikal. Founded in the 17th century, near the border of Mongolia, it has always been a key stopover on the trade routes to China. It is a beautiful city that has sometimes been described as the 'Paris of Siberia'. But, as was usually the case, I didn't get to do much sightseeing. I had the task of winning the national title, which I duly did with five straight victories. I was now well on the way to my first great international challenge, the Olympic Games. But there were still a few obstacles to be hurdled.

I DIDN'T LOSE THE FIGHT, BUT...

The pinnacle of all amateur sport — if you could call the way boxing was conducted in the Soviet Union and the Warsaw Pact nations amateur — has always been the Olympic Games. Just to go to the Olympics is the dream of every sportsperson. To go with a chance of winning is a feeling out of this world. I was no different to anyone else. I had set my sights on the Seoul Olympics in 1988, but I very nearly didn't get there. It seemed as if some of the boxing officials in Moscow were conspiring to keep me from representing my country. I was determined they wouldn't stand in my way.

My journey to Seoul had really begun the previous year at the World Junior Championships in the Cuban capital of Havana. I really enjoyed my visits to Cuba. This was my second time after the training camp in 1986. Russians were very popular thanks to the propaganda put out by Fidel Castro's government. After all, sugar was the country's biggest export and the Soviet Union bought much of it at highly inflated prices to help the Cuban economy. We were staying in the centre of Havana and the staff of the Soviet Embassy showed us around and took us to some of the best restaurants in the city.

Boxing is a major sport in Cuba and we knew the stadium would be packed for all our fights. This was to be my last hurrah as a junior, so I was determined to make the most of it. There were only 13 fighting in my division, so I would only need three bouts to win the title (although I knew it would be difficult if I came up against a local boy in the final). Fortunately I did get a relatively easy run through.

In my first bout I came up against the Bulgarian Dimchu Boev. I knew he was good but known to be a bit of a wild man in the ring. I was determined to put pressure on him from the first round and score points with my counter-punching. The fight opened as I had planned. Lots of jabbing. In the second round I knocked him down with a solid right to the head. He got back to his feet but I knew I had him. In the third round I caught him with a left to the liver and a right hand to the head. The referee stepped in and stopped the fight.

In my semi-final I was matched with Eduardo Rivas from Panama. He was a very tall left-hander. Like Boev, he was a bit wild and liked to throw a flurry of punches hoping to catch his opponent off guard. Again the fight went according to plan. I chased him and herded him into a corner where I went at him with all-out attack. I hit him with a left hook and a right punch underneath the ribs, then a right hand to his head knocked him down. In the second round Eduardo tried to take the initiative, but I counter-punched, a flurry of about five or six heavy blows. I then threw a right underneath quickly followed by a left hook and it was all over. The referee stopped the fight.

In the final I came up against the Cuban Juan Hernandez, one of the finest boxers ever to lace on a glove. It's just a pity that being

Cuban he never got the chance to box professionally, for I'm sure he would have become a world champion in the paid ranks. Hernandez had already won a previous amateur world junior championship. He was a lanky, strong left-hander. At 191 centimetres he was one of the tallest boxers I have ever encountered. I was giving away a lot of height and reach. My head only came up to his chin. He had won three fights to get to the final beating Kwon Man Deuk (Korea), Arpad Szasz (Hungary) and Olaf Trenn (East Germany).

I knew Hernandez was a very sharp puncher. His most dangerous weapon was a right to the liver, which only the finest of lefthanders could use to good effect. I would have to watch out for that. I believed if I was to win I would have to make him come to me and work on getting in lots and lots of punches — overwhelm him with the number of my blows. I wrote in my diary: 'I have to win impressively so that the judges don't have the chance to go the other way and the Cuban fans don't have an excuse to dispute the decision.'

It was a close fight. I hit Hernandez with a lot of punches, just as I had planned to do, but he continually held on to me to stop the barrage of blows. I think this should have told against him in the scoring, but it didn't. I was sure I had won, but the judges thought otherwise. Ever since that day I've wondered about that result. The Cubans have always complained about what they see as unfair decisions in places like the United States and Korea. But boxers from other countries have always joked that to beat a Cuban boxer in Cuba you have to knock him out. Needless to say I was devastated. I thought I had done everything required to win, but the gold medal went to Hernandez. I have a standard reply when anyone asks me about losses like that to Hernandez: 'I can't say I lost the fight. But I didn't win it.'

It was the one and only time I fought Hernandez, so I never got the chance to go for revenge. He continued fighting in the amateur ranks right up to the Sydney Olympics in 2000. He went on to win the senior world championships in the welterweight (67 kilogram) division in Sydney (1991), Tampere, Finland (1993), Berlin, Germany (1995) and Houston, Texas (1999) as well as the so-called world championship challenges in Tampa, Florida (1992), Dublin, Ireland (1994) and Macon, USA (1995).

Hernandez's victory in the 1999 tournament shows just how crook the judging of amateur fights can be. He was 'beaten' in the final by Timur Gaidalov of Russia — a decision so blatantly wrong that the Cubans walked out. But after a top-level inquiry Hernandez was later given the gold medal and four of the judges were suspended for four years for what was described in the inquiry's report as 'gross and blatant divergences'. That is as near as saying cheating as I've ever heard.

Hernandez won a silver medal at both the 1992 Barcelona and 1996 Atlanta Olympics — his defeats in the finals being the two of only three losses in five years. At the 2000 Sydney Olympics the Cubans also protested after he lost a controversial quarter-final bout to Kazakhstan's Yermakhan Ibraimov. Hernandez retired a few months later because the amateur rules state that once you turn 34 you cannot continue to fight at the Olympics or World Championships.

When young men in the Soviet Union turned 18 it was compulsory to serve in the military. So it would be with me. Being an elite sportsman you were fast-tracked into one of two military establishments — one to become an officer in the army and the other was for a similar role in the secret service, the KGB. As sportsmen you either belonged to the Army sporting group or Dynamo, the KGB sporting group. I joined the latter before my 18th birthday. But because of a complicated system, where you could not take the oath of allegiance until you were 18 but you could not be in military college without swearing the oath, I actually spent only 20 days in uniform — from July 20 to August 8.

I was later sent to a training camp at the Black Sea resort town of Alushta, the so-called 'Gateway to the Ukranian Riviera'. It's on the Crimean Peninsula, just 40 kilometres east of Yalta. This is where American President Franklin D Roosevelt, British Prime Minister Winston Churchill and Soviet dictator Josef Stalin met near the end of World War II to decide on the spoils of victory after Hitler's defeat. Nearby is the port of Sevastopol, home to the Soviet Black Sea Fleet and, at the time I was at Alushta, off limits to visitors — even the local population — because of the secrecy surrounding the fleet.

Alushta is a beautiful place with the backdrop of the magnificent Mount Demerdzhi. Anyone who sees it soon realises why it has always been a favourite spot for many of Russia's finest painters seeking inspiration. All Soviet sporting organisations used to send their elite athletes to Alushta because of the temperate climate. The Russians no longer do so. It's all a matter of money. Since the breakup of the Soviet Union, the Ukranians charge them a lot of money for the privilege, and the coffers are not as they used to be when winning world sporting contests meant everything to the Soviet hierarchy.

I returned home from Alushta in September 1987 in a terrible state. I had contracted a virus that attacked my liver, which was terribly swollen and extremely painful. I spent two weeks in hospital, much of the time on a drip. When I came out of hospital I was still in a real mess.

I was supposed to get ready to fight in the Soviet Union National Cup, an invitation-only event at Khabarovsk. This is an industrial city in the far east of the nation just 35 kilometres from the Chinese border, the second-last stop on the Trans-Siberian Railway before Vladivostok. None of the Russian boxers really wanted to go to the tournament as it was a mammoth journey for little reward. You were on a hiding to nothing. In my case I was expected to win. If I were to lose, I could forfeit my chances of making the Olympic team. I was so sick I couldn't have fought anyway. The powers-that-be thought differently.

'I'm sick,' I pleaded.

'We don't believe you,' came the reply. 'Come to Moscow and we'll check you out.'

So I went to the Soviet capital and underwent tests at the Moscow Medical Institute. I was armed with the medical reports from the hospital in Serov. But the doctors refused to look at them

'You're as healthy as a lion,' the doctor who checked me out snapped at me. 'You're bluffing when you say you're sick.'

The Moscow Institute cleared me to fight. I refused, went home and suffered the consequences. I suppose, at a pinch, I could have travelled the 5000 kilometres to Khabarovsk, stepped into the ring and got beaten. But I stubbornly held my ground.

As punishment I was booted out of the Soviet national team and my wages were immediately cut off. My stubbornness had cost me dearly. I was in limbo. I was still a boxer, but with no ranking and no financial support. How could I hope to make it to the Olympics now?

That stubbornness proved to be a godsend. I was determined officialdom would not grind me down. I promised myself that my fists would get me to Seoul. There were several tournaments that would make or break me.

The first was at Leningrad (now St Petersburg). An international competition at which there were fighters from other Eastern bloc countries as well as the best of the Soviet boxers. I won all my fights to win the tournament. In the semi-final I beat a fighter named Kolesnikov, who had won the Khabarovsk event. In the final I beat another Seoul hopeful Gerik Nyrkazov. But apparently I had not yet served my penance. I was still not back in the national side despite my victories.

The next step was the Soviet National Championships in January 1988. They were held at Tashkent, the capital of the Uzbekistan Republic. This was the first of the real Olympic qualifying events. And I was in high spirits despite the fact that there were some great boxers vying for selection, including Kolesnikov and Nyrkazov.

I won the silver medal, beaten in the final by Orzubek Nazarov, who was to later turn professional and become WBA world lightweight champion. I believe he had won the previous three Soviet titles. Again I thought I should have had gold. I was convinced the officials had it in for me. He had three easy fights against lesser opponents on his way to the final. On the other hand I had to beat three former European champions to make it through.

Next hurdle was a traditional USA versus Soviet Union tournament. I won my bout. In the same tournament the great Roy Jones Jnr beat my good mate Alexander Lebzyak, who later won gold in the light-heavyweight (81 kilogram) division at the 2000 Sydney Olympics. In Seoul, March 1988, I won the pre-Olympic tournament, easily beating the East German Andreas Zuelow in the final.

My last chance to gain selection for the Olympics came in June at a tournament in Leningrad. I was 'beaten' in the semi-final by another fine Cuban boxer, Julio Gonzalez, even though I knocked him down and almost senseless in the final round. Nazarov was already through to the final and the Olympic selectors wanted to see how each of us fared against the Cuban. Nazarov lost all hope of going to Seoul when Gonzalez utterly destroyed him. By the way, Gonzalez was to go on and make a name for himself in the amateur ranks, winning the World Championship in Moscow in 1989 and the World Championship Challenge in Berlin a year later.

As far as I was concerned I was riding high after Leningrad.

Suddenly I was back in the national team. I was going to take on the world's best at the Olympics.

Then came a terrible setback. Just 17 days before the start of the Games I was training just outside Serov. It was at an all-round camp, with cultural as well as physical pursuits. One evening I was acting in a play when a glass wall at the side of the stage suddenly shattered. A sliver of glass sliced through the little finger on my left hand, severing the tendons. I was rushed to the Moscow Medical Institute where doctors stitched up the gaping wound and then considered what to do. They told me that normally they would have placed my hand in plaster for at least a month. But the Olympics were too close. There was even a suggestion that they should amputate the entire finger. A drastic step, the logic being that the wound from an amputation would heal quickly enough for me to compete in Seoul.

Memories of that moment came back to me years later when in 2002 there were stories in Australian newspapers and on television about a footballer, Daniel Chick, who took such a step. Chick, who played for Hawthorn in the AFL, had his left ring finger chopped off at the first joint because it was affecting his ability to catch the ball. A dislocation made it difficult when he leaped in the air to take a mark.

'Everyone was a bit shocked,' Chick told journalists. Of course they were. I know my family, friends and fellow boxers would have been just as shocked if I had gone ahead with such a radical solution to ensure I competed at the Seoul Olympics.

Eventually the doctors decided the plaster would come off in four days at which stage I would begin exercises to enable me to use the hand when punching. Some herbalists prescribed a special cream to rub on several times a day, and within a week I was in the ring sparring. The finger hurt like hell every time I punched, but I was determined to fight in the Olympics — come what may.

I knew I was taking a big risk, but that stubborn streak of mine showed again. As it turned out, the finger never recovered properly. A decade and a half later I still cannot clench it properly and because the nerves, as well as the tendons, were severed it remains numb. The other members of the team knew about my predicament, but it was kept secret from my opponents. When I was in public I removed all the bandages.

Despite the setback I was still supremely confident. I was competing in the lightweight (60 kilogram) division. And the man who had beaten me in Leningrad, Julio Gonzalez, wouldn't be there since Cuba was boycotting the Olympics because the Castro Government refused to recognise the status of South Korea as a legitimate nation. To them there was only one Korea, the Communist north. North Korea, Ethiopia and Nicaragua also boycotted the Olympics.

Although my left hand was usually my most potent weapon, I decided, whenever possible, to use my right instead. In my first bout I knocked out a Filipino named Cantancio in the first round. The next bout was against the British boxer Sean Knight. Again I brought my right into use and the referee stopped the bout and crowned me winner in the opening round. The field was now down to 16 boxers. I was feeling more confident than ever when I was matched with the man I had beaten in March in the pre-Olympic tournament in the same Seoul arena — the East German Zuelow. I thought I had done enough to win easily and so did those in my corner. Two judges gave me the nod, another two reckoned Zuelow had won and the fifth judge, Abdul Hani of Iraq, scored it a draw. However, under the convoluted Olympic rules when scoring a draw, a judge still has to designate a winner, in case there is a split decision like in my bout. Hani gave the fight to Zuelow. I couldn't believe it. The German went on to win his next three bouts and the Olympic gold medal, beating Sweden's George Cramme in the final.

I was extremely disappointed, as I thought I had done enough to win. I was even more shocked when I later discovered that the South Koreans regarded me as one of their own, because my great-grandpapa was a Korean. They had promised every Korean who won a gold medal $1 million. Who knows what would have happened had I been given the judges' nod and taken Zuelow's place as gold medallist? One million dollars! I most surely wouldn't have ended up in Australia. Maybe I would be living in Korea today. Isn't life funny?

The judging of the boxing at the Seoul Olympics left a lot to be desired. Early in the tournament a Korean, Oh Kwang-soo, lost a controversial bout in the light-flyweight division to American Michael Carbajal. There was uproar. But not as much as the next day when a New Zealand referee ordered two points to be deducted from the score of Korean bantamweight Byun Jong-il. This resulted in Byun losing the bout to a Bulgarian. There was pandemonium, with Koreans, including a couple of security guards, jumping in the ring and manhandling the referee. Once the ring was cleared Byun sat down in silent protest for more than an hour. Unfortunately it didn't do any good.

There was a real case of daylight robbery in the light-middleweight division when Korean Park Si-hun benefited from no less than five hometown decisions to win the gold medal. The worst of the five was in the final against Roy Jones Jnr, regarded by many experts as the greatest fighter pound-for-pound in the history of boxing — amateur and professional. He toyed with Park. It seemed as if he didn't want to embarrass the Korean by knocking him out. After the fight one American television network checked out the punches and found Jones had landed 86 to Park's 32. To the astonishment of everyone, the judges gave the bout to Park 4-1. Park even apologised to Jones through an interpreter, saying: 'I feel very bad.'

The outrage of the boxing public around the world forced a change in the rules for judging amateur bouts. From Seoul on each judge was given two buttons — one for the boxer fighting out of the blue corner and the other for the red corner. Whenever a scoring punch is made, the judge pushes one of the buttons. If a majority of the judges push their buttons simultaneously a point is scored. This way everyone knows who is winning.

Some of the judges are so senile that they have trouble remembering which button judges which boxer — and others are so slow that their votes never register in time. And I have often seen judges holding only one button. They have already decided which boxer is going to win ... no matter what happens in the ring.

My greatest disappointment came after I lost. As if I wasn't distressed enough, once I got back to the Olympic Village I was told I was going to be on the next Aeroflot plane home. I wasn't alone. Four other Soviet boxers who had lost were in the same boat, or should I say, the same plane. We hadn't even had time to get out and enjoy the Olympics. We had wanted to go to the Food Hall and try out all the foreign foods available. We had wanted to go out and mix with the local people, to buy presents for our families back home. We had even arrived stocked with tins of caviar to sell on the black market. Caviar was relatively cheap back home. In Seoul you could make $30 or $40 profit on every tiny can.

Why were we sent packing so quickly? I can guess at the reasons. We had been promised $30-a-day allowances but had not been paid during the three weeks we were there. What happened to that money? And when we got to the airport we found we had only been given the tickets for the trip to Seoul. The tickets for the return journey had disappeared. But the Aeroflot officials didn't bat an eyelid. They just put us on the plane back to Moscow as if nothing had happened. It was all very, very strange.

It wasn't only the officials who were out to make money. Some boxers would make enough money on the black market during one overseas trip to buy a new car when they returned home. But to do so they would have to work hard at buying and selling while they were away — and that meant getting beaten in their first fight. They would travel with a couple of suitcases full of cameras, clothes, caviar and Russian toys. And if they were winning their bouts they wouldn't have time to sell them. Bangkok, for the King's Cup tournament, was a real favourite. They could use the profits from the Russian goods they sold to buy T-shirts for $1 each and make a 1000 per cent profit once they returned home to Russia. I saw some boxers arrive in Bangkok with one suitcase and have six suitcases on the return journey. Imagine how many T-shirts were packed into those bags. They might earn enough for that new car — but it would usually be their last trip. The trainers frowned upon it.

I would make two or three overseas trips a year — but was never a real businessman. I went away and fought for my pride and reputation. I came home with little. That's not to say being a boxer on the national team wasn't a lucrative profession by Russian standards. I was able to save a fair bit of money during my career.

One day when I was about 18, Papa pulled me aside and explained that he had a chance to buy a new car. A Lada, of course, the only brand ordinary Russians could buy. He had put his name on the waiting lists several years earlier and now he had reached the top. I suspect he bribed an official to make sure he got there a bit quicker than normal. Papa did not have all of the money. Unless he paid the 9000 roubles the next day, the car would go to the next person on the waiting list. At a wage of 300 roubles per month he had no hope of saving that kind of money. Luckily I had been able to save almost that much. And with a bit of help from three or four mates I was able to pay for the car the next day. The Tszyu family was overjoyed.

We were just as excited as years later in Australia when a sponsor gave me a new Bentley worth more than a house. The Lada was a lot cheaper to run than the Bentley that needed $100 worth of petrol every couple of days.

Back in Serov I was to make a decision that would make me stand out from the rest for years to come. I decided to show my individuality by arranging to have a unique haircut. A mate and I went into a hairdressing salon in the centre of the city and he chatted with the hairdresser for a while as they decided what should be done to my hair. They decided I should have one tuft of hair at the back that was longer than the rest — a sort of mini-tail. And that's how the characteristic tail that remains with me today came about.

There have been stories about how I grew it for strength, like Samson in the Bible. That's all just journalistic exaggeration. I just wanted to be different. At first it was just several strands of long hair that hung loosely down my back. Later, when it grew longer and I wanted to keep it tidy during my fights, I arranged to have it plaited. My family used to do it. Now even I can plait my 'tail'. It's been called everything from a rat's tail, to a pigtail to a ponytail. To me, it's just 'my hair'.

LOVE IS IN THE AIR

I put all the disappointment of Seoul behind me as I focused on what would be the most important year, so far, in my career. In 1989 there would be both the European and World Championships at which to test my mettle. The European titles were being held in the Greek capital of Athens. It was yet another great city to which my boxing career had taken me — the cradle of European civilisation. Home of the great philosophers of history such as Socrates and Aristotle about whom I had read so much. And the site of the first modern Olympic Games.

I was fighting in the lightweight division and it proved to be perhaps my finest tournament yet. I beat the Romanian Daniel Dumitrescu in the semi-final. He was a prize scalp. At the Seoul Olympics he had won his way through to the final, where he went down to Italian Giovanni Parisi. It was a real feather in my cap to have beaten the Olympic silver medal winner who, incidentally, backed up at the Barcelona Games in 1992 to reach the quarter-finals.

In the final at Athens I came up against the German Zuelow who had beaten me under such controversial circumstances at Seoul. It was our fourth encounter during our careers. This time I won easily on points. So pronounced was my victory that, as well as the gold medal, I was named Boxer of the Tournament. For some reason I was given two trophies for this. Why, I will never know. It was just one of those strange things in sport.

Mentally, I was riding on the crest of a wave when the World Championships were staged in Moscow. The European title success had really buoyed my spirits and I easily cruised through to the semi-finals where I was to meet my old foe Zuelow again. It was there that disaster struck. On the eve of the semi, I came down with an awful case of diarrhoea. It was so bad I thought that someone had poisoned me. Maybe they had — stranger things have happened at some world championships.

I was also quite foolish in that I went sightseeing on the morning of the fight. The chance to visit the Russian Diamond Fund, a famous museum in Red Square, was too good to miss. The museum housed some of the finest gold and platinum artifacts and some of the world's biggest gemstones including sapphires and diamonds. The gold exhibition, that included a huge nugget named Mephistopheles, did little for me. But I was amazed at the diamonds, especially the 190-carat Orlov diamond. It was given to Catherine the Great by her lover Count Orlov when she took over the throne of Russia after having her husband assassinated in 1762.

It was an exciting morning, but I arrived back at the hotel a couple of hours before my fight, utterly exhausted. The diarrhoea had taken its toll. I should have stayed in my room and rested. Yet, I still put up a good show against Zuelow. He won on points by just

17-14. He then went on to lose the final to the Cuban Julio Gonzalez, the fellow who had beaten me in contentious circumstances before the Seoul Olympics. The world championship final was controversial, too. Gonzales and Zuelow finished equal on points, 15-all. Somehow on a count-back, the Cuban was given the verdict.

At the time an Australian boxing trainer, Johnny Lewis, had watched me in action in Moscow and was very impressed. What he told his friends back in Australia was to change my life forever.

About this time I first got involved with Natasha. I first knew her as Natasha Anikina, a hairdresser who worked in a salon in Serov. She was three years younger than me. It wasn't a romance like Australians would imagine. There was no love at first sight. Natasha and I were part of a group of teenagers who would go out together for a bit of fun. Gradually Natasha and I got to see much more of each other, without the rest of our friends, and I realised she was something special. I couldn't wait to see her each time I came back to Serov from a tournament or training camp with the national squad. Deep down I knew that she would eventually be my wife and mother of my children.

I led a pretty mundane life until I met Kostya. My father (Leonid) was a truck driver, my mother (Valentina) was a nurse. Ironically, she had gone through nurses' school with Kostya's mother and they worked at the same hospital in Serov, even though the families lived in different suburbs. I had never met Kostya until I started working as a hairdresser in the centre of Serov. I would head into the salon at 6am each day, but after work a few of us would go for a drink and we ended up in the same group as Kostya. Of course, he was quite famous. Everyone in Serov knew what a great boxer he was. I never in my wildest dreams thought we would end

up together — me a shy, simple girl earning a few roubles as a hairdresser and him the famous sportsman with plenty of money (by Russian standards). From the first day I always wondered what made him tick. He was so polite, always punctual, things that I admired. And there was no ego. Among our group he was our equal. A mate. A friend. After a few months things began to get quite serious and he took me away for my first adult holiday to visit some distant relatives of his in Tashkent. His sister Olga went with us as a 'chaperone' so my family wouldn't be outraged. After all, young people in Russia never went away together alone. It seemed only natural that when he eventually decided to move on to continue his career overseas I would go with him.
— *Natasha*

Sometimes I've been pushed into a corner and forced to use my fists outside the ring. Luckily these times are few and far between.

One that sticks in my memory was the time Natasha and I were larking about on the sofa. It was in 1990, not long after we met. We were a bit boisterous and she fell off the sofa and gashed her right knee. It was a deep, ugly wound that has left a scar which she still carries today. We ended up in the emergency ward of the local hospital. I knew most of the doctors, having been patched up on more than one occasion after a bout. I was worried about Natasha losing too much blood so I went looking for one of the doctors who knew me in an attempt to jump the queue in the casualty ward. But the only doctor around was a fellow I had never seen before. I was to find out later he was from another city and in the short time he had been at the hospital had attained a reputation as a bit of a bully. The staff had been too scared to complain about him.

This fellow was acting the tough guy. He was about 45 years old and a lot bigger than I was. He ordered me into an office with a curt 'Let's go and talk!' When he closed the door behind the two of us, with Natasha still outside, I started to wonder what he planned to do. I soon found out as he started snarling and literally pushing me around the office. I always worried about using my fists outside the ring. After all they are lethal weapons if used as such. But I wasn't going to be shoved around by this arrogant bully. I hit him with a few hard punches to the face. It was too easy. He had got away with browbeating people in the past and was not equipped to handle someone who could fight back. He went down like a sack of potatoes. Just then the door opened and a woman, who I later discovered was the hospital superintendent, asked what was going on. The doctor got to his feet, with blood pouring from his nose and from cuts on his lips and forehead.

'Nothing,' he replied. 'The floor was slippery and I fell down cutting open my head.' She gave him a quizzical look, turned on her heel and walked out without saying a word. She knew exactly what had happened but was not going to follow it up.

Apparently, because he was from out of town, the doctor did not know who I was. When he did realise he came, cap in hand, and asked if I would teach him how to box. I just stared at him and shook my head. He didn't learn from the incident — a few weeks later he was transferred back to his hometown in disgrace. He was a bully to the end.

I'm not proud of what I did that day, but I will never allow myself to be pushed around — be it by an arrogant bully of a doctor or by an overbearing government or sporting official or, indeed, anyone.

GOODWILL TO ALL MEN

As far as achieving my full potential ... I am still a relative novice in the boxing game.

I was to get my chance to avenge my defeat at the Seoul Olympics on a truly international stage in the 1990 Goodwill Games in Seattle, a city in the north-west of the United States.

The Goodwill Games were the brainchild of American television mogul Ted Turner (owner of CNN) who tried to build a bridge between East and West after the boycotts of the Olympics in 1980 and the events in Los Angeles four years later. The first Goodwill Games were held in Moscow in 1986. The Seattle Games were the second such gathering and there were to be further Goodwill Games at St Petersburg (1994), New York (1998) and Brisbane (2001) before the idea was scrapped.

Before the Goodwill Games I won a tournament at Simferopol, the Crimean capital in Southern Ukraine close to the Black Sea. It's an historic city of around 350,000 people and the site of the ancient kingdom of Scythia and its famed ruler King Skythur. I wrote in my diary at the time of my success there: 'As far as achieving my full potential ... I am still a relative novice in the boxing game. It is like when a sculptor goes to work. He starts with a rough piece of marble knowing that eventually by chipping away at all the rough edges he will finish with a beautiful sculpture. So it is with me. I am still little more than that roughly hewn piece of marble. The finishing touches are still a long way from being applied.'

This sculpturing continued in Seattle. The Goodwill Games were by invitation only. Only the crème de la crème of amateur boxing took part. I fought in the junior-welterweight (63.5 kilogram) division, in which six other boxers had also been invited. As is the luck of the draw, I was given a bye in the opening round — the quarter-finals. My Soviet teammate Aleksandr Banin beat Korean Lee Jae-Hyuk (a Seoul Olympics bronze medal winner) on points. American Terronn Millett stopped East German Joerg Heidenrich and another fighter from the United States, Mark Lewis, beat Canadian Mark Leduc on points. In the semi-finals Banin beat Lewis and I easily accounted for Millett. Banin was a good fighter but had never really challenged me, and it was no different in the final, with the judges giving me the decision on points. It was not quite the Olympics — but I was still very proud when I stood up on the dais with the gold medal around my neck.

It is interesting to note that Millett, when he eventually turned professional, had two important bouts against opponents that featured in my boxing life, winning the IBF junior-welterweight title from Vince Phillips in February 1999 and losing it to Zab Judah in July 2000.

My old nemesis Andreas Zuelow was fighting in the lightweight (60 kilogram) division at the Goodwill Games but was eliminated in the quarter-finals by my Soviet teammate Mikhak Kazaryan. An interesting fighter in that division was American Shane Mosley, who lost in the semis. He was to go on to become one of the great names of the professional ranks.

In a lower division still, the super-featherweight (57.5 kilogram), the winner of the gold medal was Oscar de la Hoya. This American was to become one of the greatest of all pro fighters and was often mooted as a possible opponent when we were later both world champions.

The King's Cup in Bangkok the following year was a watershed in my life. This competition holds a lot of prestige. So my success in the Thai capital added to the kudos I already enjoyed. It was, however, an incident away from the ring that was to help shape my future life.

In Bangkok the Russian team was housed in the same hotel as the Australian squad. As a result I ran into Australian trainer Johnny Lewis and WBC world featherweight champion Jeff Fenech for the first time. I didn't know it at the time but Johnny had seen me in action at the world titles in Moscow and had been impressed. He had told his promoter mate Bill Mordey that he thought I could make it right to the top in the professional ranks. In Bangkok, he and Jeff were keeping a close eye on my performances.

I couldn't believe the riches that were available. Jeff had just made a million dollars. It was a figure that defied imagination to a fighter from Russia who would be getting around $6 or $7 a day, a total of $50 for the stay in Bangkok. I looked at the jewellery that Jeff was wearing and thought how that alone could buy a car in Russia (if you could get to the top of the waiting list). Jeff told me (through an interpreter) that, as I had already won the Goodwill Games and the European Championships, if I could win the next world title, in Sydney, I could earn big money in the West. He gave me his business card and suggested we keep in touch. We certainly did!

I had first noticed Kostya at the Moscow world championships. If you had asked me at the time whether he won or lost, I couldn't have answered. All I know is he was a standout, a winner even if he didn't end up with the gold medal. There was something about him, something I couldn't put my finger on. All I knew was that he had the potential to become one of the greatest boxers of all time if he were to embark on a professional career. I thought it would be a crying shame if he stayed in Russia without any chance of earning a dollar from his talents. I had spoken to the Russian team doctor who reckoned he was the best his country had seen in decades. What attracted my attention? I can't really say. I suppose it's like when [Brisbane Broncos Rugby League coach] Wayne Bennett sees a kid with talent playing football in some remote country town or when [horse racing trainer] Bart Cummings sees a horse enter the sale ring. They know — they just know. So it was with Kostya. I told [Sydney promoter] Bill Mordey about him. He was going to travel to Bangkok with me to have a look at Kostya, but at the last minute he couldn't make the trip. I saw Kostya win the King's Cup and was even more convinced of his incredible ability.
— *Johnny Lewis*

Johnny Lewis had told me about this exciting young Russian boxer he had seen at the world championships in Moscow. 'If we could get him to turn professional he'd go all the way,' Johnny explained, and he wasn't wrong. You only had to take one look at Kostya in action to realise his immense potential. He had incredible skills, great body movement and wonderful hand-eye coordination. I spoke to him through an interpreter and was determined to meet up with him again in Sydney at the world

championships and show him around the city. I reckoned that if we could persuade him to move to Sydney and link up with Johnny a world title would be a mere formality.
— *Jeff Fenech*

How fragile is our hold on life. One day you can be going about your business without a care in the world. The next you can be fighting for your very existence. I am reminded of this every time someone asks me about the prominent scar on my upper lip. They just assume it is a product of my years in the ring.

'In what fight did you get that scar, Kostya?' they will ask. When I tell the story they are amazed. It was in March 1991 when I was due to go to a training camp at Rodolsk near Moscow in preparation for a tournament between Russia and the United States. The camp was the domain of the elite, just like the Australian Institute of Sport in Canberra. The day before I was due to leave home an annoying pimple appeared just above my top lip. Natasha tried to squeeze it, but to no avail. We've all done it at some stage in our youth, haven't we? Squeeze the pimple or blackhead and within a day it's all cleared up.

It was a long trip, the 400 kilometres by bus to Yekaterinburg and then the plane to Moscow. On the trip the pimple began to swell and throb. By the time I arrived at the camp it was so sore that touching it felt like a red-hot poker had been stuck in my face. By the morning I was a real mess with half my face swollen grotesquely out of shape. I couldn't even open my eyes. They rushed me to a local hospital, then on to a specialist clinic nearby and straight into the operating theatre. Apparently when Natasha squeezed the pimple the infection was pushed deep into my face and it affected all my sinuses. The infection was close to affecting my brain. Doctors told me that a few hours later and I would probably have died. The prominent scar is from where the doctors quickly cut into my face to relieve the pressure of the infection. It remains as a constant reminder as to how simple things can go wrong. Such a trifling incident, but with such awful consequences. I was in hospital for 10 days.

The irony of it all was that I never once received a scar during the 270 bouts I fought as an amateur. I went to America for the tournament, but was in no condition to fight, I just watched from ringside as my countrymen had a workout in preparation for the European and World Championships.

I defended my European title in Gothenburg (Goeteborg), Sweden, in May 1991. The tourist brochures describe the city of Gothenburg, the second largest in the country (after only Stockholm), as 'Sweden's Friendliest City'. The people were just so wonderful, and, what was even better, I came away flushed with success. I was confident. It had been two years since I had been beaten, and I couldn't see any name among my opponents that truly worried me.

I was to contest five fights within the space of a week. My opening bout was against a Scottish boxer, James Pender. He was not very good and to be truthful I could have knocked him out in the first round had I chosen to do so. I decided to use the fight as a more intense sparring session and we went the full three rounds. The final point score was 21-0 in my favour. The bout freshened me up. In my second bout I knocked out Englishman Darren McCarrick in the first round. Attila Arshan from Turkey lasted just two rounds in our quarter-final fight. I then beat a Yugoslav named Dobrozinovich to set up an encounter in the final with (who else but) Andreas Zuelow. It was to be our sixth and last fight. It was a real tussle but by the end of the second round I had broken him physically and went on to win quite convincingly on points.

I wrote in my diary about the way I felt when standing on the winner's podium: 'It is so great to stand on the top of the dais. Quite frankly I can't get enough of it.'

Not only did I make amends for Moscow — I was named Boxer of the Championships, just as I had been at Athens two years earlier (and again received two trophies). I now set my sights on that elusive world title.

ON TOP OF THE WORLD

8 November 1991. A 26-hour flight from Moscow was almost over. The Sydney Harbour Bridge appeared under the plane and I was in awe of the scene that unfolded below me. The azure blue of the harbour, the white sails of the Opera House, the silver windows of the skyscrapers reflecting the sun and the deep green parks of the city. Sydney, Australia. This was to be the Russian team's home for the next month as we tried to win world boxing titles for our homeland of Russia. As usual, as it was the national team, Chernya stayed behind in Serov, waiting for news of my progress to be shown on Russian television.

We were driven from the airport to the Rushcutters Bay Travelodge, next to the beautiful harbour, and once in my room I opened my diary and made my first Australian entry. 'I'm tired,' I wrote. 'I'll write down my first impressions of Australia tomorrow when I've had a good night's sleep.' I never did get to put pen to paper about those impressions. But, a decade later, I remember they were good, very good! They had to be, for they would help persuade me to make this country my new home.

We had our first look at Sydney the following day — a Saturday. Just a stroll up to Kings Cross where I experienced my first fast food meal in Australia It was a Big Mac eaten at McDonald's in the main street of the Cross. It might sound pretty mundane to most Australians, but it was a big deal for a kid from Serov in Siberia where there were no such things as McDonald's or KFC or Pizza Hut.

The team would go for runs in the park adjacent to the hotel and gaze in wonderment at the hundreds upon hundreds of expensive yachts moored in the harbour at the end of the park. I didn't know it at the time but these were the yachts owned by members of the Cruising Yacht Club, famous for organising the annual Sydney to Hobart Yacht Race, one of the most gruelling events in the world. I could only wonder how people could be so rich as to afford these sleek ocean-going boats. As well as the runs we would work out in the gym and relax with games of football in the park or cards in the hotel, and I had my usual arguments with the trainers. What's new!

On the Wednesday we moved to the Novotel at Darling Harbour within walking distance of a popular area for tourists and locals alike. There was the nearby Entertainment Centre in the Haymarket area in the city, the venue for pop concerts and sporting events, Chinatown and its many restaurants, and scores of other restaurants and tourist shops scattered around the foreshores. Thursday was my Mama's birthday but, as members of the team, we weren't able to phone (only those who won a gold medal were going to be allowed that privilege). I managed to persuade a Russian television crew who were there following our progress to allow me to send my birthday wishes. The video clip was shown on national television back home, and Mama had a little cry when she saw it.

Forty-nine countries were represented in Sydney. In my division there were 24 boxers and I was the hot favourite. Local newspaper reporters and photographers had been buzzing around me. They were particularly intrigued with my haircut. Predictably, I was asked over and over again if I was trying to be like Samson, and I just laughed and tried to explain how I was just trying not to conform.

 With a Korean grandfather and long hair cascading down the back of his neck, Konstantin Tsziu [sic] is a Russian boxer with a difference.

Twice voted the No. 1 boxer in the European championships, he will be a star turn in a light-welterweight division brimful of talent in the world amateur titles starting tomorrow.

With the barriers of Communism now shattering into tiny pieces, Tsziu can speak quite openly about his desire to seek a professional contract after next year's Barcelona Olympics.

'He will go wherever he can get the best contract,' said a Russian team official. 'He has had a number of offers.'

We spoke to the sounds of rattling speedballs, the grunts of fighters slamming the heavy bags and skipping ropes smacking the floor in a makeshift gym on the fifth floor of what is now the shell of the old Government Printing Office.

Boxers from half a dozen countries made threatening growls, whooshes and snorts as they shadow sparred in three rings.

— *Sydney* Daily Mirror *reporter Terry Smith*

Of course, not being able to either speak or read English, I knew none of this, and I knew nothing about 'a number of offers'. I was soon to find out about one solid offer in the coming days.

Among the 24 in my division was the one fighter from the host nation, Australia. Shannan Taylor. I didn't know him and he made an early exit, beaten by a boxer from Ghana in the first round, but our paths were to cross again in the future, although not in an official bout. Another to drop out early was the German Zuelow. He beat a Dane in the first round but then fell to an English boxer. I had hoped he would have gone further and we could have met once again, so I could avenge the defeat at the Moscow world titles.

My first opponent was a Mexican named Albertano Caballero. I didn't know what he even looked like, let alone how he would fight. I was feeling good, despite a mild bout of the flu. I fought well, overwhelming the Mexican until his seconds threw in the towel in Round Two. Two days later I was back in the ring again, up against the Puerto Rican Anibal Acevedo. He was a wild fighter with dozens of his punches whistling past my ears without connecting. One of his punches landed on one of my kidneys — a low blow that stirred me into an angry reaction. I knocked him down and won easily. I seemed to attract frenzied fighters. My semi-final opponent, Moses James of Nigeria, was also a wild puncher, but I managed to stay clear of his ferocious attack and win my way through to the final. Now just one bout remained between me and the gold medal.

My diary entry for Thursday, 21 November was important for two reasons. Firstly it explained my physical wellbeing and secondly it made mention of an important approach, although I didn't realise its importance at the time.

'Today every muscle in my body is hurting,' I wrote. 'And my right elbow is damaged. I have torn a muscle or ligament and it is very painful, but the good thing is that I have two days in which to recover.

'My trainer told me the news that I might have to stay in Australia longer than I thought. Apparently Jeff Fenech wants me to train with him with a view to turning professional and making my professional debut on the undercard of his world championship fight, but seriously, I don't really have any desire to do this. It's not in my plans for the future.'

On the day of the final, I walked around the hotel thinking about the offer made by Fenech. Had I been forced to make a decision then and there I would have said 'No'. After the world championships I really wanted to have a good, long break. I didn't want to start training immediately, and I wanted to get home to my family and friends. I was missing them. I would flick through their photographs in the album I brought with me. The thought of them back home wondering about how I was going provided the inspiration, the encouragement, the incentive to do well. I wanted the gold medal to take home. But I was not ready to completely reject the offer from Fenech. The thought that a group of Australians were keen for me to stay, maybe for good, did have some appeal.

I wrote in my diary: 'If they offer good money I might decide to stay. The people are so different. But that is because they have freedoms that we in Russia can only dream about. They have a laid-back lifestyle that is hard to comprehend.'

The biggest fight is the one within yourself. You must get rid of any negative thoughts or emotions. You must always be positive.

I nearly didn't get to fight for that coveted gold medal. After the semi-finals the team managers announced that all the boxers who had been beaten were going straight home to Russia. The officials had been told by their bosses back in Moscow to cut costs. As team captain, I proposed that the five of us who had made the final of our division should forfeit. We'd tell the management that if some boxers went home, we would all go home. Imagine the furore that would have caused, with five finals having to be cancelled. The international media would have had a field day. The Russian boxing chiefs would be embarrassed in the eyes of the world. I suggested our plans for a boycott be put in writing. Everyone stayed in

All rugged up against the Soviet winter. As a baby with Mama

I was about three when this photograph was taken

Kids having fun. With a neighbour, when I was about four years old

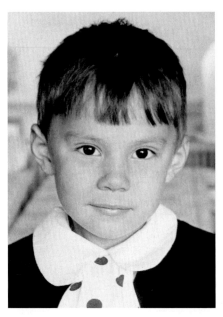

At six years of age, butter wouldn't melt in my mouth

Olga and me. At least *she* has a hint of a smile

Schoolmate hopefuls (left to right) — Salavat, Oleg, Andrey, Arsen and me, with trainer Vladimir Chernya (far left)

The first steps to greatness — the first three medals I ever won

Military service in 1987 — a brief interruption to my boxing career

Catching up on my chemistry studies for my university/army entrance exams

Showing off. But if you could lift 24 kilograms with one hand, wouldn't you?

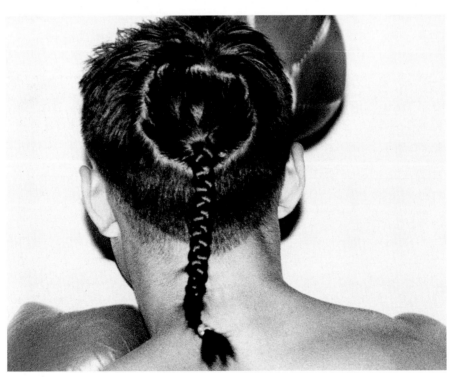

My trademark hairstyle. It wasn't to be like Samson — I just wanted to be different

Beaten for the 1988 Soviet title by Orzubek Nazarov, who later turned professional and became WBA world lightweight champion

Off to training camp   posing with Mum, Olga, Vladimir Chernya (wearing a tie) and friends

Best of mates … with my two close friends, Arsen Galoustyan (left) and Andrey Kondratev (centre), at the forest training camp where I almost severed a finger just before the 1988 Seoul Olympics

Cooling off

Bound for Seoul … with coach Vladimir
Chernya at Khabarovsk, venue for my
final training for the 1988 Olympics

A break in training for the 1989
European Championships

Константин Цзю — чемпион Европы-89.
Весовая категория 60 кг, г. Серов

The spoils of victory … after success in the 1989 European Championships, with my gold medal and two trophies as the best boxer of the tournament

Miserable Moscow memory — defeat by Andreas Zuelow in the semi-finals of the 1989 World Championships

Sydney, or everyone left for Moscow, but the team preferred face-to-face negotiations with the management. I knew this would be a waste of time, but that's what we did. The team managers told us the return tickets had already been bought and that they would lose money if they cancelled out. I now know this was utter bullshit. We even offered to spend the rest of the visit in the hotel so as not to run up any further expenses, but were told that wouldn't help. The lie about the costs convinced the boxers not to go ahead with the boycott and we went out to the airport to say farewell to our less fortunate mates. I knew exactly how they felt. I had been in the same boat at the Seoul Olympics. I was devastated back then, just as they were shattered this time.

This all provided unnecessary tension on the eve of the finals, and I am sure it affected the way most of the Russians fought. I had been through so many skirmishes with officials that I was able to block the whole affair out of my mind, but a few of the others obviously couldn't handle the anxiety it had caused. The other four Russians who had made the finals were all beaten.

I am finally the best on the planet. It wasn't the best fight in my career but ...

I was to fight the 20-year-old American Vernon Forrest in the final of the world championships. History has shown what a good fighter he is. After our meeting in Sydney he was destined to be beaten in his first bout at the 1992 Barcelona Olympics by Britain's Peter Richardson. Forrest would go on to turn professional and, in late 2001, win the IBF world welterweight championship and, early in 2002, add the WBC crown.

The Americans had always provided some great fighters in this division, so I was particularly wary of Forrest. He was tall, around 182 centimetres (just under 6 feet in the old measurements), and I noted in my diary how he liked to get in close and attack. My plan was to work on counter-punches to unsettle Forrest. Another diary observation was: 'Here I am one step away from the ultimate goal and I feel nervous. Indeed, I haven't felt this nervous for a long, long time, but in my sport the biggest fight is the one within yourself. You must get rid of any negative thoughts or emotions. You must always be positive.'

I had trouble sleeping on the night before the final. After several hours of tossing and turning in my bed, I managed to nod off around 2am, but the fretful night did not seem to affect me. I wrote one last note in my diary the morning of the fight: 'Even without sufficient sleep, *I feel great!*'

The fight, as in all my recent bouts, went according to plan. I had little trouble from Forrest despite his height and spirit, and the judges gave me the greatest victory of my career.

Daily Telegraph columnist Jeff Wells summed up the fight:

> His performance against Forrest was extraordinary. Kostya simply stood in front of him, defied him to land a punch and gave him an awful beating. [It] reminded me of Australia's great turn of the century lightweight Young Griffo who would stand in a bar — where he spent most of his time — with his feet planted on a handkerchief and defy any comers to land a punch on his head.

I knew nothing of Young Griffo, but I knew how to avoid punches and that knowledge had won me a world championship. I added a few words in my diary that evening: 'I am finally the best on the planet. It wasn't the best fight in my career but ...' I never completed the sentence. I didn't need to.

Once I won gold I tried to drink a victory toast, but the nerves conspired against me. My throat was swollen with nervous excitement and I couldn't swallow. I eventually telephoned Mama and Papa in Serov with the good news. I had some even more exciting news for them, but that could wait until I got home to Russia. I had decided there and then to turn professional.

It wasn't a hard decision to make. Over the years since that world championship success, journalists have attributed words to me about how disappointed I was at never having won an Olympic gold medal. The implication was that I regretted not continuing on with my amateur career and competing at the 1992 Barcelona Olympics. Nothing could be further from the truth.

Standing on the winner's podium in Sydney I realised I had climbed to the top of the mountain. I couldn't go any further. An Olympic gold medal? Well, it would have only equalled what I had achieved in Sydney, not bettered it. I stood on the dais and knew I had nothing left to prove.

| THE ROAD TO GOLD AT THE WORLD CHAMPIONSHIPS | | | |
State Sports Centre, Homebush, Sydney			
17 November 1991	W KO2	Albertano Caballero (Mexico)	
19 November 1991	W Pts3	Anibal Acevedo (Puerto Rico)	
20 November 1991	W Pts3	Moses James (Nigeria)	
23 November 1991	W Pts3	Vernon Forrest (USA)	

State Sports Centre, Homebush, 1991. Bill Mordey and Johnny Lewis have just watched young Russian Konstantin Tszyu befuddle slick American Vernon Forrest to win the world amateur title at junior-welterweight.

Both men know they have seen a special talent.

Mordey, Australia's leading promoter at the time, wants to add Tszyu to his stable but has to convince the Goodwill Games gold medallist and three-time European champion to turn his back on likely glory at the 1992 Olympic Games.

The next day a meeting is set up, and Mordey takes the naive Russian, who has no more than a smattering of English, to lunch at glamorous Doyle's [Restaurant] at Watsons Bay.

The sun is shining on the harbour and Mordey has asked for, and got, the best table in the place.

Mordey, always a canny operator, then pays for drinks for several of the diners, who casually stroll over, as requested, to pat Tszyu on the back and congratulate him on his success.

Overwhelmed by the surroundings, the offer of money unimaginable in his bleak Siberian hometown of Serov, and the astonishing number of people who apparently recognise him after his triumph, young Tszyu signs on the dotted line.

And while Tszyu's relationship with Mordey eventually soured … the now undisputed junior-welterweight champion of the world does not regret the decision he made that day.
— *respected boxing writer Winsor Dobbin in the* Sun-Herald *newspaper (2002)*

Soon after the win, I met with Sydney promoter Bill Mordey, trainer Johnny Lewis, former world champion Jeff Fenech and a few others. They urged me to join their group and fight in Australia. They talked about the opportunities that Australia offered. They didn't need to spell that out. I could see the opportunities every which way I looked. Opportunities I would never hope to have in Russia, but I was still in the clouds after my success. My mind was not clear, not able to say yes to the $10,000 bait being dangled in front of me for my first fight in the Mordey camp. $10,000! A king's ransom for a kid from Serov.

They say everyone has his or her price, and journalists have suggested I was overwhelmed by the thought of the money being offered. They pictured me as a kid still wet behind the ears being bedazzled by the riches of the West. But money wasn't the reason that I decided to turn professional. It was just that there was nothing left for me in the amateur ranks. I had not lost a fight since Zuelow beat me in the 1989 world titles in Moscow, and in the meantime I had found I could win most competitions without training properly. I was spoiled. It was all too easy. A breeze. It had happened in Sydney. I had been unable to sleep the night before the final but still beat the best in the world.

Yet I knew deep down that this over-confidence would be my undoing. The day would come that I would make a mistake. The lackadaisical training schedule would prove to be my undoing and I would lose a tournament. It would happen, probably sooner rather than later.

I told Bill I would probably accept his offer but wanted to think it over and persuade Natasha to come with me. He handed me $1000 for expenses and told me he would arrange tickets for both of us to come to Sydney.

After returning home to Serov, and thinking long and hard about what I was going to do, I decided that I needed to start a new life Down Under. And what a roller-coaster ride it would be!

There was a whole group of us at Bill Mordey's home in Coogee when Kostya agreed to come to Australia. Bill called me over and asked: 'Lord, can you give us one of your introductions for Kostya?' I stood up in front of the dozen or so who were there and did the honours. It went something like this — 'Ladeeez and gentlemennnn! Introducing, in the red corner, from the Siberian city of Serov, the reeeeemarkable Russian rapier whose punishing, pugilistic predisposition, sensational Soviet sporting stamina and fantastic, ferocious flair will ultimately lead him to the world championship … the Prince of Pain … Kostya Tszyu!' Of course, Kostya didn't understand English … he didn't know what I was saying, but he sensed it. He truly sensed it. When I pointed at him and announced his name, he leapt to his feet and threw his arms in the air with his fists clenched, and that cheeky smile of his spread over his face. Forget about the hours in the gym. Forget about stepping into the ring. At that moment he had become a professional fighter.

— boxing expert and ring announcer, the late Ray Connelly (dubbed by his mates 'The Lord of the Ring')

THE THREE MUSKETEERS

The three who helped entice me to Australia were real true blue Aussie characters.

Bill Mordey was a knockabout ex-journalist who used to write sport, including Rugby League and boxing, for the old *Daily Mirror* newspaper. He could very well have come from the pages of a Damon Runyon novel. And like any true Runyonesque character Mordey had his nicknames. Once upon a time his mates used to call him Blue Gum. This came from a story he once wrote about a broken-down boxer named Blue Gum Matthews, who was so down on his luck that he couldn't even afford a pair of boxing boots. So he fought in bare feet.

Later Mordey turned to boxing promotions, and soon everyone knew him as Break-Even Bill. The reason was obvious. If you asked him how much he made from a fight night he would always give the same reply: "I'll be lucky to break even, mate!" Of course he certainly did more than break even after promoting several Aussie boxers who won world titles.

Bill was a chain-smoking, laconic bloke who drank bourbon like others would drink tea or coffee — and never showed a hint of it affecting him. He was forever telling journalists just how good were his boxers. His face never revealed any emotion — happy or sad. It was something that was said to have won him many a poker game. Bill later went into horse breeding in the Hunter Valley near Newcastle. Again he would tell journalists how the racehorses he bred were going to win the Melbourne Cup or other big races like the Golden Slipper Stakes. As yet, none have. But there is always next year.

Johnny Lewis was Australia's greatest trainer of boxers. Not in terms of the number of kids who had been under his training — but by their success. When I met him he had schooled two world professional champions — Jeff Fenech and Jeff 'Hit Man' Harding (WBC light-heavyweight champ).

For more than 30 years Johnny worked as a signwriter for the Sydney County Council. He had also been involved in boxing for the same time, having learned to fight in 1957 at the age of 13 in the Newtown Police Boys Club in inner Sydney. The gym was near his home in the rough, tough suburb of Erskineville. He was taught by a trainer called Dick O'Connor and never lost a fight while Dick was in his corner. When Johnny was 17, O'Connor left to look after a member of his family who was ill and never came back. Lewis took over as trainer simply because he was the oldest kid in the squad. That gym was where I was to start my professional career.

I would say my greatest asset as a boxing trainer is that I genuinely care for my blokes. Not just in the ring but outside as well. Money is not important. The greatest reward is after a fight when a young bloke puts his arms around me and says, 'Thanks,

Johnny.' And you know he means it. There is further reward when years down the track you run into someone you've trained as a youngster and they've made a good fist of life. I reckon I've helped more than a few kids stay out of jail by harnessing their anger and expressing it in the boxing ring instead of on the streets of Sydney.
— *Johnny Lewis*

Jeff Fenech, the son of Maltese immigrants, was one of Australia's greatest boxers in the history of the sport. He had been the victim of one of those awful decisions that have plagued the Olympics. In the flyweight division at the 1984 Los Angeles Games he scored a first-round knockout of Rene Centallas of Bolivia and followed it up with an easy victory over Tanzania's David Mwaba. He then came up against Redzep Redzepovski of Yugoslavia and the judges gave Fenech the fight 3-2. But, inexplicably, the match jury reversed the decision, announcing Redzepovski as the winner 4-1. Redzepovski went on to take the silver medal, beaten in the final by American Steve McCrory.

Fenech was so angered by the decision he immediately turned professional where he was dubbed 'The Marrickville Mauler' because of the Sydney suburb where he lived and his no-nonsense style of fighting. Jeff proved how wrong the amateur officials were by going on to win world titles in three different weight divisions — the IBF bantamweight (after just six months and seven bouts), the WBC super-bantamweight and the WBC featherweight crowns, and he achieved some self-satisfaction by beating McCrory with a 14th-round knockout in 1986. Several years after his retirement Jeff was to be honoured by inclusion in the International Boxing Hall of Fame.

As I was about to join the ranks of the professionals Jeff was still smarting over a 'hometown' decision in Las Vegas the previous June. He had attempted to win another world title, in a fourth weight division, challenging the WBC super-featherweight champion Azumah Nelson. Fenech was clearly the better fighter, but the official verdict from the judges was a draw.

I felt quite confident that were I to choose to pursue a professional career in Australia, the help of these three Aussies would be vital. Through a translator Bill had explained to me: 'We're all family here, Kostya. Like blood brothers.' Family? It sounded good!

FAREWELL TO MOTHER RUSSIA

My last involvement as a boxer with the amateur system of Russia occurred on the way home from Sydney. The team flew into Moscow, from where each of us would head off to the far-flung corners of the country. Of course, every part of the country was not serviced by daily flights, so we went to the Hotel Sport in the centre of the capital where we would stay until we could catch our planes home. The hotel had been built for the 1980 Moscow Olympics but had been taken over by the Sports Ministry. There was hardly equal treatment for each member of the world championship team.

Within the world championship team each member was treated differently dependent on his success. As boxers we were given somewhere to sleep. As the winner of a gold medal I was given my own room, but the trainers ... well, they were out of luck. They had to sit around the hotel lobby, some for up to two or three days, until it was time for them to fly out. It was incredible. Here was a world championship team — but the Sports Ministry was too mean to give the trainers a bed in which to sleep. What a slap in the face. One of the trainers slept on the couch in my room, but most of the others weren't so lucky.

If I had any doubts about accepting Bill Mordey's offer to move to Australia, they were quickly dispelled by the happenings at the Hotel Sport in Moscow.

I had anticipated no trouble in getting permission to leave Russia. It wasn't like the bad old days of the Cold War where elite Soviet sportsmen or women or top artists like Nureyev had to 'escape' while on an overseas tour. The barriers had come down and there had been a flood of boxers heading to the United States and Japan. Later they would migrate to Europe because it was closer to home and easier to get back for family visits. I was the first who had decided to go to Australia. The Sports Ministry gave me the green light. They knew they couldn't stop me so they wanted us to part on good terms.

It was time to prepare for the journey. I wrote a list in my diary of what I would take to Australia. Number One on that list was Natasha. She was a priority. I knew how I felt about her, and I knew that I would not be able to cope in Australia without her. I went to her parents to explain all this. I didn't really ask their permission to take her with me. I told them she was coming. At 22 years of age, I thought I was very grown up. Of course, I wasn't. I was still just a kid, but no one could tell me that. Young men always think they know better than their elders.

Natasha was just 19. A year out of school, she had never spent time away from her parents, and really, neither of us knew much about the other. We had been boyfriend and girlfriend for some time, but we hadn't spent much time together. I had always been away at training camps or boxing tournaments. We'd spend a few days together each time I returned, but a lot of that time was spent in the company of our friends. It wasn't like in the West where young kids moved out of the family home and set up life together in a flat. That was impossible under the Soviet/Russian system — even if you could have afforded to lead a separate life to that of your parents.

There I was, $1000 in my pocket, a small fortune in Russia, and ready to take on the world. The rest of my list of things to take was straight forward:

- Photos/documents/diary;
- Clothes;
- Tape recorder;
- Icons (I never went anywhere without these religious artifacts);
- Bible;
- Books to read;
- Tickets;
- Money;
- First aid kit;
- Toothbrush, razor, etc.

It may seem pretty mundane to people in the West, but one has to realise that in Russia, unless you took everything with you, you would probably have to go without the items you needed. Even if you had the money to buy them, you would not necessarily find a shop that had these apparently everyday articles in stock.

Natasha and I celebrated Russian Christmas on 7 January and then headed to Moscow where we would pick up our visas from the Australian Embassy. For some reason there was a delay and we were all packed up in the hotel a few hours before our flight was due to leave when I finally went to collect them. I left Natasha with our bags sitting in the hotel foyer. There was some last-minute hitch in the paperwork. When I hadn't returned when I said I would, she had panicked and taken a taxi to the Sports Ministry. For the next couple of hours we were rushing to and fro across Moscow trying to find each other. I also had the Russian team doctor, one of the few people I knew in Moscow, running around trying to discover what had happened to her. When we finally met up, back at the Sports Ministry, more by luck than good management, Natasha was crying her eyes out. We made it to the airport with just an hour to spare.

The trip to Australia was little more than a blur. We were so stressed out that we had a couple of drinks and that almost knocked us out. The first thing I remember is our arrival in Dubai to change planes for Singapore and then on to Sydney where we arrived on 10 January. What a contrast to what we had left behind. In Serov it had been minus 35 degrees. In Sydney it was plus 35 degrees. Bill Mordey had booked us into the Quay West Apartments near the Harbour Bridge. We had never seen anything like it in our lives, a sensational view out over Sydney Harbour, ornate furniture we'd only seen in books about millionaires. A normal Russian would have had to have spent a year's salary for a one-night stopover at a place like this.

I quickly jumped into training with Johnny Lewis at the Newtown Police Boys Club. Afterwards Natasha and I would wander around the shops in the centre of Sydney. It was a real eye-opener for Natasha, she could hardly believe that if you had the money you could buy anything you wanted. Not like back in Russia where you had to put your name down on a waiting list for luxury items. Our big problem was finding familiar food and drink items. It is surprising how many supermarket items don't have pictures on the label showing what is inside the packet or tin, and we couldn't carry a Russian–English dictionary around with us when we went shopping. We tried 15 different wines before we found one that we liked. It was a bit like a holiday at first — but that would soon change. On 17 January 1992, I wrote in my diary: 'Life is so boring. I am glad that I have my training. Once you've walked around the city there is little else to do.'

The following day was one of the most significant of my life, but

I would not realise this for several years. It was the day I signed my contract with Bill Mordey. The contract seemed so unimportant that I didn't even bother to mention it in my diary. I'd never signed a contract in my life. In Russia there were no such things. The government ran everything. If they got tired of you, you were discarded. You were not able to fight them in the courts. Even if you had been able to do so, the government would always win. I just did what I was asked, signed the contract and thought nothing more about it.

Knowing what I do today, I would have been straight off to a lawyer and gone through each sentence with a fine-toothed comb before I ever put pen to paper!

LOST IN THE TRANSLATION

*He has the eye of a hawk, the heart of a lion and
the strike power of a cobra.*
— Johnny Lewis

D-Day was 1 March 1992. I was to make my professional debut against the Queensland junior-welterweight champion, Darrell Hiles, in the open air at Princes Park, the home ground of the Carlton Aussie Rules football team in Melbourne.

Darrell and I were on the undercard to a bout in which Jeff Fenech was challenging Azumah Nelson for the WBC world super-featherweight title. As I mentioned before, they had met previously for a controversial draw in Las Vegas. It would be a great baptism for me in front of a huge crowd of screaming fans. They didn't know me, but Jeff had told them through the media to come along and cheer for the 'next Aussie who will win a world title'. I could hardly speak a word of English. I had been here for less than two months, but already Jeff had made me an honorary Australian.

I knew nothing about Hiles, the fellow I would fight in my first professional bout. However, I was told he was a handy sort of fighter. He was an Aboriginal boxer from Queensland who had suffered only one defeat in his eight professional appearances — and that was to Grahame 'Spike' Cheney, who had won a silver medal for Australia at the 1988 Seoul Olympics — the Games that had proved so disappointing for me. Hiles had also represented Australia at Seoul, in the featherweight division (57 kilograms), the one below me. I never saw him fight, but the records showed he had beaten a Turk by the name of Celikiz in his first bout but then was out-pointed by eventual bronze medal winner, South Korean Lee Jae-hyuk.

I got to see him on video for the first time 10 days before the bout. I wrote in my diary: 'He's tall, with a good left hook. If it weren't my first professional bout he wouldn't provide any problems, but it will be the first time I have fought over 10 rounds [as compared with the three rounds of amateur boxing]. Ten rounds is a long time.' People said I was crazy to agree to have my first fight over 10 rounds. I was convinced I was ready. Such is the brashness of youth. I couldn't sleep properly the night before the fight. I had put unnecessary pressure on myself. I need not have tormented myself for, despite all the apprehension, deep down I knew what would happen. Once again on the morning of my debut I wrote: 'Another four hours and part of my life's history will have unfolded. Everything is depending on this day. But everything will be fine. I have prepared so well that I cannot fail.'

My English was still virtually non-existent. I had an interpreter ringside, but he didn't have time to translate Johnny Lewis' final instructions as the bell rang for the start of the first round. I thought Johnny had told me to win the fight in the opening round. So I did. Poor Darrell Hiles didn't know what hit him. Bang, bang, bang! It was all over in less than a minute. The victory had certainly come my way much quicker than I had expected.

Back in the dressing room, I asked Johnny [through the interpreter]: 'Why was it so important that I win the fight in the first round?' My trainer just shook his head in bewilderment: 'I didn't say that. I told you to make sure you *won* the first round. You had another nine in which to win the fight!'

If there is a golden rule about watching Kostya Tszyu box, it may be simply this: do not blink, and do not get up for a few minutes in search of a hot dog with mustard, as I did just before the young Russian climbed into the ring for his first fight at Princes Park. By the time I resumed my seat, complete with sausage and sauce, there was no sign of the lad. He was back in the Carlton footballers' dressing rooms having despatched Queenslander Darrell Hiles in precisely 58 seconds.
— *Ron Reed of the* Herald-Sun *newspaper, having missed a part of history*

I'll be one very disappointed person if Kostya doesn't win a world title. He has the eye of a hawk, the heart of a lion and the strike power of a cobra. Talk about potential? Kostya Tszyu has the potential to win a world title within 18 months. He's a kid in a million.
— *Johnny Lewis*

I was well pleased with myself. My professional career had got off to the best start possible, but overall there was doom and gloom in the Lewis camp that night. Jeff Fenech lost his fight with Azumah Nelson, with the world champion stopping him in the eighth round. His career was winding down. Mine was just beginning.

DARRELL HILES
Queensland junior-welterweight champion
8 bouts, won 7, lost 1
Australian Amateur Champion (57 kg division) in 1987
Olympic representative at Seoul in 1988

Career record (at the time of our fight)		
21 April 1990	W KO7	Ray Ludham at Toowoomba, Qld
1 June 1990	W Pts10	Lance Austin at Toowoomba, Qld
21 July 1990	W KO5	Troy Power at Toowoomba, Qld
15 September 1990	W KO5	Troy Power at Goondiwindi, Qld*
22 April 1991	L KO10	Grahame 'Spike' Cheney at Blacktown, NSW
2 June 1991	W Pts10	Simon Maidment at Broadbeach, Qld
10 August 1991	W Pts10	Albert 'Kid' Binoa at Honiara, Solomon Islands
13 December 1991	W Pts10	Sovita Tabuarua at Kogarah, NSW

* won Queensland junior-welterweight title

Natasha and I returned from Melbourne to Sydney after the fight and we were like two excited school kids. Under the terms of the contract we had signed, Bill had promised to provide us with furnished accommodation for 12 months. He said he had found a nice apartment, but we wanted to have a dog and the owners of most flats refused to allow pets, so we asked if he could find us a house instead. Neither of us had ever lived in a house before so it was going to be a new experience. I asked that any house be near a park so I could go for my daily training run. We wanted to have a shopping centre nearby and we didn't want to be far from the beach That was for two reasons — to relax when I wasn't training and to have swimming as part of my training regime.

We arrived back from Melbourne at night and were driven to our new home in O'Riordan Street, Mascot. The address meant nothing to us. The names of suburbs were just that ... names. The house itself was a big comedown from the luxury of the Quay West, but we were expecting that. Bill had scrounged second-hand furniture from members of his family and friends, but that didn't worry us. It was as good, if not better, than we had been used to back in Russia. There were two bedrooms and a small backyard for our yet-to-be-purchased dog. Natasha and I had each other. We now had a house. We were as happy as we could be.

There was no food in the house, so that night we went out looking for some shops. We walked and walked and walked, this way and that but couldn't find anything. Eventually we found a service station and bought a couple of sandwiches that we ate on the way back to the house.

We went to bed, weary but happy. Our new life in Australia as a self-sufficient couple had begun. At about 5am we were awoken as the house began to shake. The first semi-trailer was roaring past our bedroom window. An hour later it was bedlam. What we discovered was that O'Riordan Street, Mascot was located slap-bang in the centre of one of the biggest industrial areas of Sydney with scores of factories, serviced every day by hundreds of trucks, and we were only five blocks from Sydney Airport, with the planes coming so low over our house that you could almost reach up and touch them. There was no shopping centre. There was no beach, but there was Mascot Park, a soccer ground opposite the house, where I could run.

That first morning, we just looked at each other and laughed. What else could we do? We had little money. We had this weird house in a strange location. We had someone else's furniture. But we were young and in love. That was all that mattered, and we had the friendship of the people in Bill's office. That motivated us to stay. We set about making the most of the situation.

Talk to the animals

I've always loved animals. In our little flat in Serov we used to have a tiny dog we called Malishka (Russian for 'petite one'). In Sydney Natasha and I were determined to have pets around us, too. Hence the house in Mascot.

Our first dog was a Rottweiler. We named him Viking and he's still with us today. The breeder we bought him from on 16 February 1992 was a Macedonian named Jim Gestakovski. He understood a bit of Russian and helped us out in those first traumatic months. We have become very good friends.

We've since added to our menagerie. We purchased a Lhasa Apso, a small, long-haired Tibetan dog. We called her Malishka, after my old dog in Serov. We had an Electus parrot named Leha. I was teaching the parrot to talk, but sadly, in 2002, the day I came back from one of my fights in America there was a loud noise outside our house, Leha was frightened and flew off (her first-ever flight). She was never seen again. We have plenty of fish in a tank and were planning to add some turtles and frogs. The most exotic of all our pets was a baby python. We called it Jake the Snake after one of my opponents (and later a good friend). Who knows what other breed of animals will eventually become part of the Tszyu household.

Life was littered with simple problems. I wanted to get a driver's licence, but to get that you have to have several forms of identification. A passport wasn't enough. The officials asked for details of a bank account. But when we went to open a bank account we again found a passport wasn't enough. Show us your driver's licence. It was all Catch 22.

Language (or lack of it) was the biggest problem. Bill enrolled us in an English school in Bondi. Most of the other students were Japanese who had a smattering of English. We had none. We had to search for every word in our English–Russian dictionary. After the first lesson, the teacher separated us because we were conversing with each other in Russian. I was put on one side of the room, Natasha on the other. It was so difficult, so frustrating.

People who have never lived in a foreign country can never understand the nightmare of not being able to ask the simplest of questions and understand the simplest of answers. Where is the toilet? Will this bus get me to the city? May I have a ham sandwich, please? What day is the garbage collected? And what about shopping? Many products do not have pictures on the boxes to help you. How do you tell the difference between a box of headache tablets and one for flu? It was even more difficult for Natasha. She had virtually never been out of Serov. To her, Sydney was like another planet. Once the holiday atmosphere of the first month was over she was distraught. She was so homesick. I told her how much I needed her — but I also pointed out that if she left to go home it was the end of our partnership. I told her that this is our life, our future. We must come through it together. It wasn't easy. She had to be strong.

It was a real shock for me. I had lived at home all my life, relying on my parents to do everything for me. While we were at Quay West Apartments it was like a vacation. Now we were back in the real world — and a very different world to anything I had ever experienced. I had to learn to cook. The house had to be cleaned. Shopping was a nightmare because I couldn't speak English and the foods were all so different to back in Russia, and we were in a strange city without any friends and no local knowledge.

Bill Mordey tried hard to make us happy. And Brian Mills from Bill's office was our 'driver'. He was a real darling. Sometimes you feel uncomfortable with people who speak in a different language, but never with Brian. He would drive us to and from training every day. He would chat away in English. We didn't have the slightest idea what he was saying. But you could tell from his face he wanted to be our friend. Later when we could speak a bit of English we told him how much his happy smiling face meant to us in those dark early days.

We tried to keep very busy. It would have been very easy to stay at home, turn on the television and hope that by watching the pictures you make some sense of the program. But we would have ended up as hermits. Instead we tried to keep busy. We started our English lessons. There were the daily training sessions. We took part in aerobic classes at the South Sydney Leagues Club three or four times a week. Sometimes we would stay on for a second class — anything to stop us going back to our lonely home. Gradually people became our friends.

But I was still terribly homesick. I had only been away from Serov on a couple of occasions in my life. I remember when I was about seven or eight years old going to visit some distant relatives at a place called Zaporozhye near the Black Sea (my Mama wanted me to get some sun, and there was precious little sun in Serov), and the time when Kostya once took me on a visit to Tashkent. But I had never been away from home as long as this.

I cried many, many nights. It was tough for Kostya, too. But he has this incredible self-will. He understood my unhappiness and eventually he said to me, 'If you want to go home I will buy you the ticket. But it will be a one-way ticket.' He also explained he really wanted me to be with him. 'Be tough,' he implored me. I couldn't imagine him being by himself in this strange city. So I was tough and stayed, and each of us gave the other the support needed to get us through those difficult times.

That traumatic period helped build my confidence. If I could get through all that, I could get through anything. So, when I turned to study, nothing was going to beat me. First learning English. Then learning the basics of computers. I felt so dumb at first — and it was hard working with an English keyboard when my native language was Russian. But I triumphed. Then it was a course in business. I remember sitting for an exam in Business Law. Everyone else in the course was Australian-born, so the essays were relatively easy for them. I managed to write the required essays and passed with flying colours. Yes, I am very proud of what I have accomplished in my studies.

— *Natasha*

13
A NEW FRIEND OUT OF THE BLUE

It was on the night of my professional debut that I first met Vlad Warton. He had come to Australia as a teenager. His family arriving when he was just 15 with less than $100 in their pockets. They found a flat in Neutral Bay and Vlad had to fight to survive in an environment in which the other kids poked fun at his inability to speak a word of English. Because of this humiliation he was determined to do better than his peers, and within a few years his linguistic ability was such that he was out-talking the best car salesmen along the Parramatta Road strip. That was no mean feat. He was so successful that when we met he had a thriving business — Five Dock Auto Mart Quality Used Cars.

He had seen me win the world amateur crown in Sydney and had flown to Melbourne with his Australian wife Carol specially for my first fight. Vlad came up to me in the crowd and introduced himself. 'Can we meet back in Sydney?' he asked. Of course! I jumped at the opportunity. I didn't know a soul in Sydney outside the Mordey team, and here was the opportunity for Natasha and I to speak to someone in our native tongue.

A few weeks later we got together for the first time, and it was like a breath of fresh air. I've often said that Natasha and I were like two kittens, blind when they were born and needing someone to lead them, to show them the light. Vlad was that person.

We had been tied to the house. The only times we could really get away was when one of the Mordey crew drove us. Roman Lubouny, a young Russian I had met when I was here for the world championship, was working as my masseur. He took us shopping on a couple of occasions, but he had to borrow his mum's car for this to happen. We needed a car of our own.

Vlad came to the rescue, giving us our first car. It was nothing flash, an old Holden that was worth about $1000, but it was like a Rolls-Royce to us. At last we were able to drive to the big shopping centres. We'd go there and just walk around looking in shop windows. We'd go out for a drive. Where did we go? It didn't matter. We just jumped in the car and drove around Sydney, looking, finding places we had never seen before, watching how people lived in this new country of ours.

We became closer and closer to Vlad. He was like a second Papa to me. He was at all my fights. Never once did he ask for tickets. He went out and bought them like everyone else.

What he offered was his friendship. When we asked for help he was there to provide it. When we went to buy new furniture he came with us and handled all the negotiations. When we went looking for a new house to rent in mid-1992 he helped Natasha in the search, while I was busy training for a fight, and they found one, a lovely three-bedroom house with a swimming pool in Bestick Street, Brighton-Le-Sands, not far from where he and Carol lived. When we decided to buy a house, he helped us find one in nearby Sans Souci and helped with all the legal paperwork.

His friendship was such that he was concerned to ensure that we were not being exploited in the boxing game, and when he questioned deals made on our behalf he quickly came into conflict with Bill Mordey. Bill used to mumble about 'those bloody Russians'. Eventually it had to come to a head.

On 2 April 1992 I had my second professional fight, this time in Sydney against a fellow named Ned Simmons. We were pretty well in the dark about him too. There wasn't even a video of him in action. We just knew he was a Jamaican-born boxer, who lived in Toronto, Canada. He hadn't been too successful, losing a dozen of his 16 fights, but he had gone the 10 rounds on several occasions. The fight, like my first in Melbourne, didn't even last one round.

We didn't know much about Simmons. One punch did the trick for Kostya. It was a real one-punch KO — Simmons was dropped dead in his tracks.
— *Johnny Lewis*

We expected a tougher encounter for my next outing from Western Australian Tony Jones, a former contender for the Australian lightweight championship. Although he hadn't fought since losing (because of a cut eye) to Pat Leglise in a title bout almost three years earlier, he was a tough fighter who had only lost a couple of times in his career.

It was Tony's first fight for a while, but he was a very capable fighter. Kostya completely outgunned and outfought him. It went into the second [round] but Tony was only delaying the inevitable.
— *Johnny Lewis*

Johnny Lewis knew Kostya was heading for the world title after just three fights. A couple of weeks after the youngster beat Jones, he was putting on his headgear for a sparring session. Johnny called me over and said, 'Ray, we've got something very special here, he's going to go all the way to the top'.
— *boxing expert and ring announcer, the late Ray Connelly*

MY OWN OLYMPIC FINAL

I can't believe a kid with only three pro fights can
have a chance against me.
— Juan LaPorte

The time had now come for my first real test. Although my first three opponents weren't 'patsies' it was decided that I needed to fight a really tough campaigner. He was to be the veteran Puerto Rican Juan LaPorte, 10 years my senior and with a string of fine victories stretching back to 1977. He was a former WBC world featherweight champion and had been involved in no less than nine world title bouts.

LaPorte had fought in Sydney before. In October 1990, he had lost a points decision to Azumah Nelson in a bout that had been staged as a prelude to the world title challenge from Jeff Fenech, that was to take place in Las Vegas eight months later. I was determined that LaPorte's losing record in Australia would continue.

Our fight took place at the Darling Harbour Convention Centre just one day before the opening of the 1992 Barcelona Olympics on 23 July 1992. Had I not turned professional I would have been in Spain taking on the likes of Oscar de la Hoya, who was destined to win gold. Members of the media kept asking me about the Olympics and whether I regretted not being there. They just couldn't grasp that, as far as I was concerned, it didn't matter in the slightest.

'Beating Juan LaPorte will be my Olympic gold medal,' I told them. They just wrote down the quote, while shaking their heads in disbelief. The journalists also reckoned I was being overmatched. They pointed out that in winning my first three fights I had never even got into a third round. In fact I had spent a total of just 5 minutes 23 seconds in action. LaPorte, on the other hand, had boxed a total of 398 rounds during his career. The Puerto Rican had never been knocked off his feet. Backing up his toughness was the ability to score a knockout with either hand. LaPorte obviously felt the same way as the journos.

'I can't believe a kid with only three pro fights can have a chance against me,' he told one reporter, but Bill Mordey explained his predicament: 'What could I do? The kid was demolishing well-credentialled fighters and I had to find someone who could stay on his feet.'

I had studied a video of one of LaPorte's fights and wrote down the plans for our confrontation, which I knew was going to be a real test of my ability to make it in the professional ranks. I was buoyed by the fact that LaPorte had lost four of his last seven fights.

'This ex-world champion is a very good boxer. He is maybe a little slow, heavy in the legs, a one-paced fighter. I should work hard in getting some good punches in around his liver. I think, if I can take the fight to him for the first four or five rounds, he will get quite tired, but beware! He has a great right cross and a sensational left hook. Because of his experience I need to be very careful, to watch him closely. I must not rush. Instead, I should try to get some enjoyment from the fight.'

Enjoyment? What better enjoyment could I get than beating a former world champion? I knew after I caught him with some solid punches in the second round that, unless I did something stupid, I was going to win, and I was right in my pre-fight thoughts — he did get more and more tired as the fight wore on, especially when I ripped in plenty of blows to the liver as I had planned. He seemed intent on just seeing off my punches rather than trying to score with punches on me. When the bell rang for the end of Round 10, I knew I had won. I didn't need to wait for the scores to be announced.

Neither did LaPorte. He had just seven fights after our meeting and lost four of them, including a couple of vain attempts to win minor world titles. In hindsight I think I was stupid to have taken on a man of his expertise with so little professional experience behind me. I was young and unafraid and, as it turned out, LaPorte provided me with an important stepping stone in my journey to the top.

I think LaPorte made up his mind [he had no chance] at the end of Round Two. *Ring* magazine once rated him as having the best chin in boxing. He'd never been KOed. I think against Kostya he was more intent on protecting that feat than winning the fight. He really pulled down the shutters after Round Two. It was obvious he just wanted to go the distance, but that didn't worry us. It's like a marathon. You never know if you can run one until you do. Kostya needed a good long hit-out and he got one, but he won every round.
— *Johnny Lewis*

JUAN LaPORTE (Puerto Rico) World title fights		
WBC featherweight		
13 December 1980	L Pts15	Salvador Sanchez at El Paso, US
WBA featherweight		
24 January 1982	L Pts15	Eusebio Pedroza at Atlantic City, USA
WBC featherweight		
15 September 1982	W TKO11	Mario Miranda at New York, USA
20 February 1983	W Pts12	Ruben Castillo at San Juan, Puerto Rico
25 June 1983	W Pts12	Johnny De La Rosa at San Juan, Puerto Rico
31 March 1984	L Pts12	Wilfredo Gomez at Hato Rey, Puerto Rico
12 December 1986	L Pts12	Julio Cesar Chavez at New York, USA
WBO junior-lightweight		
29 April 1989	L Pts12	Juan Molina at San Juan, Puerto Rico
WBC super-featherweight		
13 October 1990	L Pts12	Azumah Nelson at Sydney, Australia

Having beaten LaPorte, I had suddenly jumped up the ratings to be No. 6 contender for the WBC world junior-lightweight crown. It was incredible. I had the experience of just four professional fights (and a total of 14 rounds) and I was knocking on the door of the ultimate prize.

Bill was determined that there should be no let-up. I was back in the ring seven weeks later on 11 September 1992. My opponent was Argentina's Daniel Cusato. We were the supporting bout to Australian welterweight champion Grahame 'Spike' Cheney when he beat Argentinian Hector Vilte on points for the vacant WBC

International championship. Bill talked up my credentials to the media: 'The WBC junior-lightweight champion [Jeff Fenech's conqueror Azumah Nelson] is the best fighter in the world pound for pound, but I'd have no worries about Kostya fighting any of the other top 10.'

Once again, I didn't know a lot about my opponent and he gave me a good workout because of his unpredictable, gangling style of fighting. I finally overcame Cusato in the seventh round but was disappointed with my performance, believing I should have finished the fight a lot earlier.

Cusato went into the bout with a very good record. He turned in a very courageous performance. He was big and gangly but was never in the fight. It went seven rounds and was a good hit-out for Kostya. When Kostya hit the throttle, he gave Cusato a big uppercut and finished him. This was an important fight because Cusato was such an awkward fighter. Finally Kostya got his chance and put in the big one [punch].
— *Johnny Lewis*

15

BLACK FRIDAY

Kostya could be a ballet dancer.
There is nothing he can't do he is so athletic.
— fellow boxer Justin Rowell

It was about this time that I brought out my family from Russia —
Mama, Papa and my sister Olga — for a holiday. I'd been in
Australia about a year and although the periods of homesickness
were becoming fewer and less acute, I still missed my family a lot.
Their arrival for a stay of six months was a wonderful pick-me-up.
I had five wins within the space of seven months under my belt and
was lined up against a very useful Puerto Rican Sammy Fuentes. It
would be good to have Papa watching me for the first time as a
professional. He had seen so many of my amateur bouts and had
been my guiding light through all those years. He could now see the
fruits of his efforts in Australia.

I had had a pretty hectic boxing schedule — even if most of the fights had ended very quickly. So I told Bill Mordey that after the fight I wanted to have a decent holiday with my family. Not just a couple of days off training like I had done after the previous bouts. We'd all get away and relax. Bill shrugged his shoulders and in his typical laconic manner replied, 'Yeah, no worries.'

I was taking on Fuentes in Melbourne on 13 November, Black Friday. The superstitious would say it was bad luck, and looking back, it probably was, because in the aftermath the first seeds of discontent between Bill and me were sown. Fuentes had a record with plenty of defeats, but he also had turned in some great performances. He had won a WBC Continental Americas championship and had lasted 11 rounds with the great Julio Cesar Chavez. Bob Yalen, American ABC boxing director, warned Mordey, 'You aren't doing Kostya any favours with this fight. Fuentes doesn't take a backward step and will be in front of his opponent constantly.'

I wasn't too worried in those days. I didn't really think about who I was taking on. I still thought like an amateur, where you didn't need to know much about an opponent in a three-round bout. When I went in against LaPorte I had only seen him fight in one video. The same with Fuentes. The rest of them I went in sight unseen. I'd have done the same even if I was coming up against a legendary fighter like Chavez. In hindsight it was a reckless way to approach fights, but I was young and, I suppose in a way, cocky. Indeed, I had ignored one of the lessons I had been taught back in Russia. Always prepare before the fight. I was making too few notes in my diary before my professional bouts and making no evaluation of my performance in the wake of each fight. One day in the future I was to pay dearly for this slap-dash approach. In the lead-up to the Fuentes fight I had been sparring with Justin Rowsell, a Barcelona Olympian and Commonwealth Games silver medal winner. Rowsell told newsmen, 'Kostya looks after me a lot, but I would hate to come up against him in a fight. I've never come up against anyone as strong or as precise in their punches. He could be a ballet dancer. There is nothing he can't do he is so athletic.'

The Fuentes fight was over almost before it had started. I went for him from the opening seconds. Journalists told me later that videos had shown I landed 15 solid blows to his head and body in the 54 seconds that the bout lasted, and in that time he was twice on the canvas. I thought the referee would have stopped the fight after Fuentes went down for the first time, but he allowed it to continue. I hit Fuentes with a few more blows and it was all over. It was the first time in his career that Fuentes had been knocked out.

Bill Mordey had a wide smile after the fight. He was telling the press that I was a mini-Mike Tyson. 'He was simply awesome,' said Bill. 'I think Fuentes paid the price for believing he was a certainty to win the fight.'

Johnny Lewis told the reporters, 'I was shocked by the result. I didn't think anyone could knock out Fuentes in Round One. I was very toey about this fight, but once Kostya gets a chance, he doesn't need another.'

SAMMY FUENTES (Puerto Rico)		
World title fight		
WBC junior-welterweight		
18 November 1989	L Pts11	Julio Cesar Chavez at Las Vegas, USA

Now it was time for us to head off for a holiday. Or was it? We were at the post-fight celebration when Bill dropped a bombshell. He told me he had agreed to a fight with the tough Mexican Hector Lopez in four weeks time. I would have to get back to training the next day. I told Mordey to get lost. I wasn't going to be fighting anyone in a month's time. I would still be having a holiday. He told me that my contract stipulated I would do whatever he said, and he said I would fight Lopez. It was our first argument, and the confrontation continued for several days. It was a case of argue, argue, argue. So much for Bill's 'Yeah, no worries.' I had learned my first lesson. Apparently, in Australia verbal agreements don't count. At least, in boxing they don't. I eventually had my way, but this argument between Bill and myself had caused the first crack in our relationship.

Once in a lifetime you see somebody who will be infinitely great. This [Kostya] is your boy. He is such a natural. From the day I first saw him fight professionally, I knew he was a monster who was cool and calculated. He's like the dux of his class. At 23, there is no telling the heights Kostya can reach.

One of his great attributes is his ability to lift when required. His controlled aggression, ferocious punching power and amazing eye-hand co-ordination have genuinely astounded me. His ability is god given. I've never seen anyone move so quickly in so many different directions. He has the amazing ability to alter a blow just two or three inches from his target. He is pure talent. Unique.

Some boxing people have criticised the quality of his opponents. Not me. Darrell Hiles was a 1988 Olympian. Tony Jones was a former Australian and international titleholder. Juan LaPorte was an ex-world champion. Sammy Fuentes fought [Julio Cesar] Chavez for the [world] title in 1989. Ned Simmons lost in Round One but said he wasn't hit by a human but by an elephant. Daniel Cusato was extremely brave, but copped a terrible beating.

Kostya has almost angelic looks, but once an opponent makes an indiscretion, that tremendous spirit emerges. I spoke to Sammy Fuentes after the fight and he was in a state of shock. Kostya destroyed him. Fuentes was traumatised. Kostya knows what he

wants and his magnificent skills will see him win a world title.
— *respected Australian boxing analyst and ring announcer, the late Ray Connelly*

Bill decided I needed to establish a reputation overseas, so arranged for my next fight to be in the American city of Memphis, most famous as the former home of Elvis Presley. My opponent was Steve Larrimore, a tall and very useful welterweight from the Bahamas. Four years earlier he had won the Commonwealth junior-welterweight title by knocking out Aussie Lester Ellis in Perth. Larrimore had since lost the title to Englishman Andy Holligan. Among Larrimore's other former opponents was the fine American lightweight and future world champion Freddie Pendleton. What happened in Memphis? I smashed him. A second-round knockout. I think he was surprised at my quickness. Like other Americans I fought later in my career he had been told I was slow — and believed what he had been told.

16

HOUSE HUNTING

It was about this stage in early 1993 that Bill decided that we should try our luck in Newcastle, the steel city north of Sydney. He reckoned it could turn into a real 'hometown' for me, and so it transpired. The Newcastle people opened their arms to me. Was it because I came from a similar city in Russia, where the major industry was the steel mills? Whatever the reason, my next fight was the first of seven that I fought there.

That first Newcastle fight was important for my future, and not just in the boxing ring. Natasha and I had decided to follow the dream of every young 'Aussie' couple and buy our own home. I wrote down our plans in the diary: 'Steps to buy a home:

    1. Borrow money;

    2. Talk to Real Estate Agent;

    3. See solicitor to draw up the paperwork.

It all seemed simple enough. Except for point number one. Sure, the bank manager was happy to lend us money, but only if we had enough for 20 per cent of the cost of the house. His attitude was — if you can't find the money, then you don't buy the house. You keep on renting. It was as simple as that.

We found a house in the suburb of Sans Souci that was perfect, but we needed $62,000 before the bank would come to the party. Since Natasha and I had been in Australia we had managed to save $50,000. Our hopes for our dream house were pinned on my first Newcastle fight. If I won I would claim $15,000. Enough to keep the bank manager happy and a bit left over for moving expenses.

The fight with American Larry LaCoursiere couldn't come soon enough. I was very confident. He was from Hastings, a small town of 12,000 people in the state of Minnesota in the north of the United States. The 27-year-old had a fine amateur record (winning 130 of 150 fights) and was unbeaten in 17 bouts, most of them in the twin cities of Minneapolis and St Paul, since turning professional three years earlier. Nine of his victories had been knockouts including five in the first round and another three in less than three rounds. In my favour was the fact he had not met any opponents of real world class.

I had been bothered by a sore throat for a couple of days before the fight. I thought that maybe I would have trouble breathing if the fight went too long. On the other hand I was hoping to give my new fans who had packed the Newcastle Entertainment Centre a good fight. Sadly it didn't even last one round. I hit LaCoursiere with a flurry of punches. A right uppercut sent him down for the first time. A left sent him down again. Finally, as he tried to come at me, I back-pedalled and hit him with a crisp left hook that finished the bout. The referee had called an end to the fight before he even hit the canvas. It had lasted just 2 minutes 13 seconds.

And we had the money for our house.

The next fight in Newcastle was staged only four weeks later and it finished even quicker than the LaCoursiere encounter. Johnny Lewis had gone over the top a bit in the lead-up to the fight, comparing me with one of the sport's legendary names.

'He'll be spoken about in the same breath as Sugar Ray Robinson,' Johnny told reporters, talking about the American boxer many believe was the best boxer in history.

We didn't know much about the next opponent, Robert Rivera. He was a southpaw. In his previous fight, four months earlier, he had been knocked out by the WBC's No. 1 contender, Rafael Ruelas. Our fight went just 80 seconds. On 18 June 1993 I dropped Rivera down after the first few exchanges of punches. He got up. I dropped him down again. As he was on his knees, his trainer and the others in his corner kept shouting at him to get up, but this time he didn't want to. He just shook his head and the fight was over.

After four one-sided bouts — none of which had lasted more than two rounds — Bill said we needed a tough fight to ensure our credibility and to give the Newcastle fans a real glimpse of what I could do. He chose Livingstone Bramble, a former WBA world lightweight champion. He was a colourful fighter from St Kitts and Nevis, the Commonwealth nation of Caribbean islands south-west of Puerto Rico.

Bill asked me to talk up the fight because of the previous quick demolitions. But I didn't need to; Bramble did it for me. Gee whiz, was he a big talker — especially about himself and how he would beat me!

LIVINGSTONE BRAMBLE (USA)		
World title fights **WBA lightweight**		
1 June 1984	W TKO4	Ray Mancini at Buffalo, USA
16 February 1985	W Pts15	Ray Mancini at Reno, USA
16 February 1986	W TKO13	Tyrone Crawley at Reno, USA
26 February 1986	L KO2	Edwin Rosario at Atlantic City, USA

I went into the bout suffering from the flu, and I had twisted an ankle during training, but was determined neither would put me off. Anyone who saw the fight would never forget Livingstone. Talk about colourful trunks and outrageous spiky hair. The fans also got their money's worth as far as the boxing was concerned. In the first round I hurt him and he retreated into a defensive mode for the rest of the fight. He had only been knocked out once in his career, when he had lost his WBA crown seven years earlier, and was obviously determined he wanted to finish our fight on his feet. He achieved that, and in doing so gave me a good hard fight.

DO AND DARE

People are surprised when they find that one of my great pleasures in life is reading. You see, the image of a boxer is of some Neanderthal creature with little more than bone between his ears. And Neanderthal Man was not known for his love of literature.

I discovered the joys of the written word when I was about 12 or 13 when my Mama gave me a book that she reckoned I would find interesting. I can't remember its name, but it was about a bloke's journey through life, his trials and tribulations. My eyes were opened. I fell instantly in love with words, and to this day I am still very much in love. I have, since that day, read thousands of books. I have a couple of thousand in my library at home, many of them classics from not only Russia but other countries as well. I have another thousand or so in Russia that I am shipping out to my new house in Sydney. One of my goals in life is to track down each edition of every work by my three favourite Russian authors.

My favourite writer is perhaps Aleksandr Pushkin, the 19th century poet, novelist and dramatist. The Tsar of Russia exiled him from Moscow because his political poems were regarded as revolutionary. He influenced so many Russians, including Tchaikovsky, who based his famous opera *Eugene Onegin* on the novel of the same name, written in verse. In a bizarre finish, Pushkin was killed in a duel in 1837 at the age of 38. Next is Tolstoy, Count Leo Nikolaevich Tolstoy. Most people know him only as the writer of *War and Peace*, the epic doorstopper of a novel about the Napoleonic War; another of his great works was *Anna Karenina*. Tolstoy was a most unusual character. Not only did he encourage the education of the peasants on his family estate of Yasnaya Polyana, something frowned upon by others of the ruling class in Russia in the mid-19th century, but he eventually became something of an eccentric. He rejected all his famous literary works, lived and worked as a peasant, and renounced all forms of war. At 82 he disappeared from his home, leaving a note saying he wanted to be alone. A few days later he was found dead from pneumonia.

The third of my favourite Russian authors is Fyodor Mihailovich Dostoevsky who was also from the 19th century. The Tsar put him in a Siberian prison camp in 1849 for writing so-called socialist propaganda. Originally he had been sentenced to death, but was reprieved at the last moment and sent to the gulag Omsk. He was pardoned in 1859, but used to get into debt and would write stories and books to ward off his creditors. One of his most famous efforts was *Crime and Punishment*, and shortly before his death, in 1881, he wrote *The Brothers Karamazov*. This was made into a Hollywood movie starring Yul Brynner and Lee J Cobb.

I have also found another more modern Russian novelist, Mikhail Afanasyevich Bulgakov, incredibly interesting. In the 1920s he wrote about the Communist Revolution in none too complimentary terms — he wasn't too popular with Stalin. Many of his works were not published until decades after his death.

I suspect that some of the beauty of these Russian writers is lost in the translation of their works into English, but I try to persuade my Australian friends to get hold of copies of these works and check it out for themselves.

I'm not just a fan of writers from my native Russia. I enjoy the works of novelists from other countries. One favourite is Alexander Dumas who wrote, among others, *The Three Musketeers*. Another is James Hadley Chase, who wrote one of the biggest selling crime novels in history, *No Orchids for Miss Blandish*. I used to think Chase was American, because all his stories were set in that country. I found out he was English and had only made two brief visits to the United States, but he used maps of American cities and books on American slang to make his novels sound authentic.

Then there is Dale Carnegie. I discovered Carnegie in 1993 while I was preparing for my first fight in Newcastle, with Larry LaCoursiere. I had picked up a copy of *How to Win Friends and Influence People*, the best-selling book by the American door-to-door salesman turned motivational expert, and was immediately enthralled by some of his suggestions about life. On 19 March I wrote in my diary: 'I have been reading Dale Carnegie and he has inspired me to write a book on my life. [Little did I know that it would be almost a decade before I finally put pen to paper.] The words of Carnegie make so much sense. In essence he says that every young man can achieve anything he wants, if he has the will and determination to do so. Only if you really want something and are determined will you achieve your goal, and from all this you can find ultimate happiness.'

Carnegie's words hit me harder than any punch from an opponent ever did. There were so many of his inspirational quotes that took away my breath. I can't remember the exact wording, but the general gist of them has remained with me in the years since I first read them. Many of Carnegie's words of wisdom were to hold true for me as I pursued my ultimate goal of becoming the best boxer in the world.

For me, books are the part of my education that I never got. I never really tried hard at school. Many subjects were not taught at all. Others had no bearing on life in general. I remember being asked to speak at my school three or four years after I had finished. There were about 600 kids in the audience and I told them like it was — that many of the things they were being taught were a waste of time, and they would realise that once they got out into the real world. The teachers were appalled. 'We asked you to come here and support us,' they complained. 'Instead you attacked us.' I explained how I wasn't attacking the teachers, but the regimented system that failed to prepare kids for the future. After finishing school at 16 or 17 years of age, many would go on to university. Then when they finished their tertiary studies the big, bad world outside would be waiting for them. These kids would have plenty of knowledge up there in their brains, but they wouldn't be prepared for their working life. Then there is the little matter of history. Who was it that said, 'Those who do not learn from history are condemned to repeat it'? In the Soviet Union we weren't taught history as such — we were taught what the Communist Party wanted us to believe happened. Even today, after reading hundreds of history books I am none the wiser as to what happened in my homeland over the past century. So many historians, Russian or otherwise, seem to have hidden agendas.

SURPRISE WEDDING

When I left Russia almost two years earlier I had taken Natasha with me without asking her family's permission. I had told them Natasha was coming with me. At the time I was a brash young man and decided I didn't need authorisation for anything I did, even to take her from her mum and dad. But now we were going back to Serov and I was going to act more traditionally. I wanted to marry Natasha, but this time I would first get her parents' permission — even before I asked her to be my wife.

Natasha was excited about the holiday. We'd been looking forward to it for some time. As it turned out, she was even more excited when she found out what I had planned for that vacation.

 It was a total surprise. It was wonderful to be back home with my family. There were lots of tears and plenty of cuddles. Then

Kostya shocked us all. Out of the blue he asked my parents' permission to marry me. Mama turned to me and asked: 'What do you say about all this? Why didn't you tell us you were planning to get married?' How could I have told her? This was the first I knew about it, but what did I have to say? Yes, yes, yes!

Kostya had already made all the plans without telling me. He'd arranged all the official documents. He had booked a restaurant for the wedding reception. The wedding would be the following Saturday, 24 September 1993.

But what about me? A girl has to look her best on her wedding day. And I didn't have a dress. I didn't have any shoes. I didn't have anything. Had he asked me to marry him before we left Sydney I could have had everything under control. Clothes for such an occasion were easy to buy in Sydney. It was a different matter in Serov. They didn't sell wedding dresses in Russian shops. You had to have them made specially. My mother and I rushed around and found a seamstress who was able to make me a dress in time. Nothing fancy — but beautiful nevertheless. Buying shoes was a different matter. We ordered some to be sent from Moscow and they arrived on the morning of the wedding. When I went to try them on, I nearly cried. They were a size too small. It was almost impossible for me to fit them on my feet. This may not sound a big deal to people in the West, but in Russia, by tradition, the groom must slip the wedding shoes onto his bride's feet. It was like in the fairytale where Prince Charming slips the shoe he found after the ball onto one of Cinderella's feet, and the couple live happily ever after.

Luckily at our wedding Kostya managed to push and shove until my feet managed to squeeze into the tiny shoes. My feet hurt so much, but I didn't care. I was deliriously happy.

We did all the traditional things. In Russia a groom has to 'buy' the bride from the local community. Kostya arrived at the apartment block in which my parents lived with his arms loaded up with presents. As he climbed the stairs the neighbours would ask him questions about me. What colour are Natasha's eyes? When is Natasha's birthday? What is her favourite food? Natasha was a champion athlete at school — true or false? He was supposed to know a lot about me to prove he deserved to have me as his wife, but tradition also demanded that he got plenty of wrong answers so he could hand over plenty of presents. Once the wedding had been performed it was off to the party. Lots of vodka was drunk. Lots of food eaten. Needless to say, it was the happiest day of my life.

Back in Australia we set about starting a family. Unlike Australians who seem to sit down and decide when they will have children, Russians believe that a marriage is incomplete without a family. It was natural that we should start preparing for our first child. In February the following year it was confirmed I was pregnant. Our lives would never be the same again.

— *Natasha*

A CLOSE SHAVE

I had my next fight just before Natasha fell pregnant. It had been my biggest break between fights since I had turned professional, four-and-a-half months out of the ring.

It was to be my first appearance on American television. The bout would be staged on 11 January 1994 in Tampa, a sleepy resort city on the west coast of Florida. Sleepy? Well, I certainly got a wake-up call when I fought Mexican Hector Lopez.

Lopez had great credentials. He had won a silver medal in the bantamweight division at the 1984 Los Angeles Olympics before turning professional. Since then he had lost only two of his 28 fights, both to good fighters. Seven years previously he had lost on points over 12 rounds to Georgie Navarro, who later challenged unsuccessfully in Melbourne for Jeff Fenech's WBC world featherweight crown. Nine months before we met, Lopez had also lost on points in a WBC world lightweight title fight with fellow Mexican

Miguel Angel Gonzalez. Lopez had also won over 10 rounds against Juan LaPorte in Las Vegas just before I beat the same fighter in Sydney in 1992.

If the Lopez fight taught me anything it was to never under-estimate your opponent. Not that I actually took him lightly, it was the way the fight developed that showed me how I would have to be wary in the future. Never have I ever felt so exhausted as I was that night. I had taken the fight to him for the first three rounds and I was well ahead on points, but for some inexplicable reason I was almost out on my feet with fatigue. My legs wouldn't move the way I wanted. My arms felt dead. My gloves felt as if they had several kilos of lead in each of them. I could hardly lift my hands to defend myself. I had never felt this way in any of my previous bouts, amateur or professional. In the corner at the end of the third round I searched for some answers from Johnny Lewis. 'Johnny, I'm tired,' I told him.

'Yes, I know ... but it's fine, Kostya,' came the reply.

It was the same after each of the next few rounds. Each time Johnny assured me everything would turn out okay. Looking back I now realise he knew the limits to which he could push me. I know that if he felt I was in any danger he would have stopped the fight and thrown in the towel. Every three minutes came the reassuring words, 'It's fine, Kostya. It will be okay.'

Lopez won the next three or four rounds. I must have had him thinking I was foxing, because he never moved in to finish me off. I can thank my amateur days (when I pushed myself so hard in training that I would vomit) for getting me through that night in Tampa. As Johnny was encouraging me with soothing words, my mind was going back to those days in the Serov gym when I would be sick, wipe the vomit from my chin and carry on training.

Somehow, as Lopez was getting on top of me, from deep down I found an inner strength. Suddenly, almost without warning, I got a second wind. I had hit the brick wall and come out the other side a new person. My arms came alive again, my feet began moving exactly the way I wanted them to move. The lead in my gloves became a power that scored points off the Mexican. Boom, boom, boom — into his face and into his ribs. I won the last three rounds and took the decision on points.

From that day on, whenever I had an opponent looking tired and ready to drop, I would think to myself, 'Remember Lopez. Remember how you felt.' I would never take any chances, no matter how exhausted my opponent looked. On the other hand, I also wouldn't relax and let my opponent back in with a chance.

HECTOR LOPEZ (Mexico)		
World title fight		
WBC lightweight		
26 April 1993	L Pts12	Miguel Angel Gonzalez at Aguascalientes, Mexico

I was back 'home' in Newcastle again for my fight against Puerto Rican Angel Hernandez, buoyed by the fact that we had met a couple of the same fighters and I had beaten them more easily. I knocked out Sammy Fuentes in the first round; Hernandez won on points. He beat Steve Larrimore with a sixth-round TKO; I had hammered Larrimore in two.

My pre-fight summations were simple: 'He is a good boxer, very tall, who changes from southpaw to orthodox at the flick of a switch. He has a dangerous right-hand punch. He will attack me straightaway, but I won't rush.'

I left nothing to chance with some tough sparring sessions. The last was so tough that I finished with badly bruised ears and had to sit around with bags of ice on them to curtail the swelling.

The Newcastle Entertainment Centre was packed to the rafters on a night that coincided with the Russian Easter, and the crowd got their money's worth. Hernandez tried to use the advantage he had in height and reach, but I ducked and weaved my way in close to inflict plenty of damage. In the seventh round, he suffered a bad gash above an eye and the referee was forced to stop the bout. I had won my 12th straight fight, and in my post-match ratings I believed it was possibly my best performance yet in the professional ranks. One more fight and I reckoned I should be able to get a crack at a world title.

ANGEL HERNANDEZ (Puerto Rico)		
World title fight		
WBC junior-welterweight		
10 April 1992	L TKO5	Julio Cesar Chavez at Mexico City, Mexico

They called my next opponent, Pedro Chinito Sanchez, 'Toro Loco' — the Mad Bull. The 29-year-old was a former holder of the WBC Continental Americas title and the WBC International crown, two minor designations that were said to give fighters greater box-office appeal. Sanchez, from the Dominican Republic in the Caribbean, had lost only one of his 30 bouts — to Oba Carr, an unbeaten welterweight from Detroit. Carr himself had beaten Livingstone Bramble three years earlier and later went on to fight for world titles against three great fighters, Felix Trinidad, Ike Quartey and Oscar de la Hoya. So it was no disgrace for Sanchez to have been beaten by a fighter of his calibre.

The Sanchez encounter, in Melbourne on 29 August 1994, was crucial in my bid to get a shot at the world championship. Everything went wrong during my preparation for this fight but I just had to put the setbacks out of my mind and carry on regardless.

If I pulled out of the fight, my championship hopes would fly out the window. A couple of days before the fight I hurt my right hand in training. I didn't tell anyone about it except Johnny. He knew the hand was injured but not how much it hurt every time I landed a punch. Then I suffered a minor dislocation of my left shoulder. Again, it was very painful, but I had to carry on. The superstitious — and I am a very superstitious person — say that bad luck comes in threes. The third impediment to my training came when I injured my left thumb during a sparring session. I thought it was broken, but I didn't get an X-ray because I was afraid of what the doctors would find. It was black and swollen. Funnily enough, it was not sore. It was just that I couldn't move it and that meant I had little power in my punches.

So I went in against Sanchez with problems with my left shoulder and both hands. This may sound macabre but, quite frankly, most boxers carry injuries into their fights. It is part and parcel of our profession. How can you expect to be punching heavy bags and clever sparring partners every day without suffering injuries?

This was scheduled to be my first fight over 12 rounds, as world title eliminators have to be fought over the championship distance. I had done my homework on Sanchez: 'Opponents say he is a dirty fighter. I think he'll try to jump on me from Round One, try to run over me like a tank would. Beware of possible low blows, lots of low blows. Don't rush! Don't try to hit too hard. That way I'll lose a lot of energy and I need to be able to fight strongly for the whole 12 rounds and explode in the last round. Counter with my right hand. Keep him at a distance. Remember, the gloves are tough, but his head is tougher. My thumb is still sore, but I don't care.' As it turned out, even carrying my injuries, I had too much firepower for Sanchez and knocked him out in the fourth round. I had been fighting for less than three years, but the stage was now set for my world title challenge.

A NEW TSZYU

It is raining. That is a wonderful omen.
Rain means good luck.

2 November 1994. My diary entry for 1 November says it all: 'Today we'll have our first child. Natasha has been having contractions for the past two days. It is about time. The baby is now 11 days overdue, but the doctor has told us not to worry. He says the baby is okay and everything is going to be fine. Natasha is in fine spirits. It is raining. That is a wonderful omen. Rain means good luck.' We went to the hospital at 4.30pm, but it was still a long, long time before Timophey was born. He arrived around 6.30 the next morning.

Kostya was such a help to me during my pregnancy and labour. He can be such a tough man in the boxing ring, but out of it he can also be a real softie — although he wouldn't like to admit it. He turned up for every parenting class, working his training around this important task. When he said, 'Natasha, if the baby comes too quickly, I can do the delivery, ' I knew he could. I wanted to have a boy for him. Men always want to have a son first, don't they? When the baby was born, Kostya's face lit up. 'Natasha, we have a son,' he said with a grin from ear to ear. He was so proud. Later he left me at the hospital to spread the good news and celebrate. There was a big party at Sans Souci that night — Kostya, Mama and Papa, Igor and Olga. Everyone got very, very drunk. What is the English expression, 'wetting the baby's head'?

We named him Timophey after Kostya's grandfather.

Kostya was very good once I brought Tim home from hospital. The first night Tim just cried and cried. Kostya took him from me, told me to rest, and amazingly settled him down. The crying stopped. He's a good father, strict but loving.

Too many people will tell you that children will disrupt your lives. Maybe so. But if you are young you find the energy to cope, and you find all the work looking after the child is okay. I like to say that even the mess they make is fun.

— *Natasha*

The added responsibility of fatherhood didn't affect me as it might a normal person. After all, I had taken it upon myself to be responsible for my whole family from the time I was a teenager. Don't get me wrong, Papa was still the head of the family, and what Mama said was never questioned. But as a leading sportsman in Russia I grew up mentally much faster than the other kids of Serov, and I was earning much more than my parents could have ever imagined. Even then I was able to look after them.

When I brought my parents to Australia just before Timophey's birthday, I vowed that they would never want for anything for the rest of their lives. I was not so much the breadwinner in the family,

I was repaying them for all the hard work they had done looking after Olga and me as children. Mama still says to me, 'May I buy such-and-such?' or 'Can we afford to buy so-and-so?' My answer is always the same, 'Mama, you buy whatever you want. You don't have to ask me. My money is your money.'

My philosophy on bringing up my children is a simple one. I plan to give my kids more of my time once I finish my boxing career. I know it is not easy for them when I am in full training. I am usually in a bad mood when I come home. I am so focused on my next fight that I push my body to its limits — and then push some more. So when I arrive home I am exhausted and short-tempered. It's hard for toddlers to understand why their Mama is telling them not to make a noise or annoy me.

Once I have my last fight all that will change. I will be there to answer their questions when they come home from school, and if I don't know the answer we will search it out together. I hope to pass on my love of books and the boundless knowledge that these books contain. I will make sure my children don't lose touch with their Russian heritage, taking them back to Serov and other Russian cities like Moscow to see how their parents and grandparents lived. They are Australians but they have a wonderful Russian ancestry.

I am determined that my children will have a better life than I did. That's why we live in Australia. I will not allow them to take anything for granted. Obviously they will be well off financially, better off than many of the other kids around them. They will realise though that they will have to earn a living and learn to respect money. From the moment they could understand, they have been given chores around the house. Tim has had the responsibility for taking the garbage bags to the outside bin. It is his responsibility and he must do it every day without being asked. Woe betide Tim if I have to remind him. It may not sound much, but he is just eight years old and must learn to take responsibility, no matter how small that responsibility may be.

21

TRIUMPH SOURED

I wanted to be an Australian citizen before I made my attempt to win the world championship, but the bureaucrats had other ideas. Natasha and I would be able to get our citizenship in March, two years after being granted permanent residency, but I had asked the Immigration Department to stretch the rules to make it official six weeks earlier as I wanted to be representing my new country when I stepped into the ring against the junior-welterweight champion Jake 'The Snake' Rodriguez at the MGM Grand Casino in Las Vegas, on 28 January 1995. After all, our son Timophey was already an Aussie, so why couldn't his parents be the same?

I wouldn't be just doing it for myself. Other Australians would be proud if I was fighting for their country. The pen pushers would not be moved. The rule is the rule, they answered. They wouldn't even take in the 13 months we had lived in Australia before being granted permanent residency. I didn't want to make a big fuss about it. Even if it wasn't official, in my mind at least, I was a true blue Aussie. I would be winning the world title for Australia.

For the first time, Natasha wouldn't be ringside to give me moral support. Timophey was only three months old, too young to travel. So Natasha had to stay at home in Sydney and watch the fight on television. It was funny not having her around. I was always hard to live with in the weeks leading up to a fight, but she never complained and was there to lift me up when I finished each day dog-tired.

The family is quite religious — especially Kostya's mama. On the morning of every fight we go to church and ask God to help him win and to make sure nothing happens to him. Kostya has his own special prayers before each fight and takes his personal religious icons with him wherever he goes. It was no different for the family this time as we all went to church in Sydney on the morning of the fight to pray for Kostya.
— Natasha

My dream was now so close to coming true. The world championship belt was there for the taking. For the first week I was in Las Vegas I couldn't sleep properly because of jet lag. I would wake up at 4am and find myself unable to get back to sleep again. It is something that doesn't happen as much these days. As I have such a strict diet and precise regimen in the build-ups to fights, I am able to offset most of the effects of jet lag, but in those days I was more slapdash in my preparation.

Two days before the fight and I was at last sleeping like a baby. For the first time in my professional career I was going into the fight without an injury of some type, but I had my usual cold. I seem to catch a cold before every fight. It is something to do with the immune system. I believe elite athletes in most sports suffer from pre-competition colds. My hot shower and massage each evening not only helped to keep the weight down, but was relaxing as well and helped ease the effects of the cold.

Bill and Johnny, however, weren't so relaxed. Just 48 hours before the fight they discovered that the Australian judge Don Marks had been sacked. Apparently, Jake's manager, a former New York policeman called Dave Burke, had kicked up a fuss and the IBF had given in to him. Burke had complained that there was no Puerto Rican judge, so there shouldn't be an Australian judge. What Bill and Johnny couldn't understand was why there hadn't been a Puerto Rican in the first place, as demanded by IBF rules. After all there were two Puerto Rican judges officiating on the undercard. At first, Bill threatened to cancel the fight altogether, but that would have been like cutting off our noses to spite our faces.

Eventually he agreed to allow a Canadian, Bernie Cormier, to join two American judges, Don O'Neill and Chuck Giampa. The referee, by the way, was also an American, Dick Steele, but Bill came up with a novel plan. He asked three respected American boxing writers to judge the judges. Ed Maloney of *The Ring* magazine, Ed Schuyler of Associated Press and Michael Katz of the *New York Daily News* would score the bout independently, and their cards would be available for comparison with the official judges'. If I lost and there were obvious differences, Bill would demand an official inquiry by the Nevada Athletic Commission. Bill stressed that he was not questioning the impartiality of the judges, but all of our team objected to the obvious manipulation of the system — especially being given only 48 hours notice of a change from a previously agreed procedure. There was an audible gasp from the 400 or so people who turned up for the weigh-in, when Bill explained what he had done. 'The trio [of journalists] are all Americans and have nothing to do with us,' he explained. 'So if there is any discrepancy the public can make up their own mind about what's gone on.'

Burke hyped up his fighter, dismissing my credentials out of hand. He said I was overrated and hadn't really beaten anyone of note. That suited me down to the ground. Hopefully Jake himself would take me for granted, too ... and suffer the consequences.

As far as I was concerned I didn't plan to let the judges have any say in the matter. I hoped to stop Jake before the end of the scheduled 12 rounds. Jake 'The Snake' was a left-hander. He had lost only two fights during his career. One was to fellow Puerto Rican Felix Trinidad, one of the finest boxers in the last quarter of a century. Trinidad beat Rodriguez on points early in his career and went on to win four world titles in three different weight divisions. The other loss was to a very ordinary American lightweight named Mike Brown. Jake had told friends he didn't think the American media gave him the respect he deserved for winning the title and for twice defending it successfully.

Even though I was sure I would win, I was still treating him with the respect due to a world champion. My pre-fight summary noted: 'He has an attacking style. I think his plan will be to try to force me onto the back foot, using his left hand often to my body. I must not rush and I must not let him get in close.' And on the morning of the fight I added the words: 'I've had a good meal and a good sleep. My muscles feel good and I feel great!'

I think Jake may have been reading what the local newspapers said about me — that my feet were too slow — and believing what he had read. From the opening bell he raced across the ring at me. Those 'slow' feet moved me out of his path and I caught him with a crisp right that sent him to the canvas after about only 15 seconds, but Jake was a tough fighter. It would take more than one solid right to take his title from him. I followed him around raining blows on him from every direction. Jab, jab, jab! Punch, punch, punch!

In the second round he caught me with his head, a clash that opened a gash under my right eye. Rodriguez rallied a bit in Round Three, but I continued my relentless stalking of my prey. I sent him down to the canvas twice in the fifth round. Early in Round Six I knocked him down again. The referee claimed I hit him while he was down and docked a point from my score. It was a ridiculous decision, but it didn't matter to me. I knocked him down another two times before the ref stepped in and stopped the fight 1 minute 50 seconds into the round. A check of the video of the fight showed I had thrown 410 punches in almost 17 minutes in the ring. No less than 168 had found their mark. Jake, on the other hand, had thrown 295 of which just 86 had connected. None of the 86 had hurt me.

I was overwhelmed by a tidal wave of emotions. After three years of determined effort the world title belt was mine. There was tremendous satisfaction for a job well done. I thought to myself, 'A great future is assured.' Had I lost it would have been the end of my career. I now know that at that time I would have been unable to cope with defeat. I would not have had the mental strength to accept it.

I walked into the dressing room with the title belt around my waist. I had that bad cut under my right eye. The eye itself was swollen and turning black, but I was a winner. Then one of the IBF officials walked in and demanded I hand over the belt. He claimed the belt belonged to Rodriguez. Normally they present a fighter who beats the champion with a new belt, but they were so sure that I didn't have any chance of beating Rodriguez that they decided to save the money needed to make a new belt.

'This belt belongs to Jake,' the IBF official said.

'No way! This is mine. I've won it and no one is going to take it away from me. How can you expect me to give it up?'

A couple of my team stood menacingly at the door and the American official slunk off. He returned a few moments later and said, 'Jake says to keep it. He says you are the champion and deserve it. You can send it back when you get the new one.'

I didn't. I kept the belt I had won off Jake and sent him the brand new one, but I appreciated his gesture and filed away in the back of my mind an idea that when I needed to prepare to fight a left-hander I would ask Jake to be my sparring partner, and I did ... for the fight in Townsville the following year against Ismael Chaves, and Jake fought on the undercard.

While I was basking in the euphoria of victory those around me were speaking to the press.

I think to beat a champion in the way he did speaks volumes for the ability of Kostya. When you're a champion, you know you're the best. That's what Kostya is, but he's going to improve. Kostya is going to be a super-duper fighter. Certainly I think he will become the best fighter pound-for-pound in the entire world.
— *Johnny Lewis*

I've been saying for the past two years Kostya is the best fighter pound-for-pound without a world title. [WBC world champion] Pernell Whittaker doesn't have the skills this guy has. He doesn't have Kostya's awesome power. No one will catch the public imagination the way he does and will continue to do.
— *Jeff Fenech*

JAKE 'THE SNAKE' RODRIGUEZ (Puerto Rico)			
World title fights			
IBF junior-welterweight			
13 February 1994	W Pts12	Charles Murray at Atlantic City, USA
21 April 1994	W Pts12	Ray Oliveira at Ledyard, USA
27 August 1994	W KO9	George Scott at Las Vegas, USA

I found out later that I had huge support back home in Australia. The pubs and clubs were jam-packed with fans cheering me on. I had sensed that in the messages I received in the hotel in Las Vegas. They were barracking for me, barracking for a fellow Aussie, albeit a fairly new one. Later, when I arrived back home, I read a column by journalist Mike Gibson written about the fight. Here are some of the things he wrote. My only complaint was that he kept calling me a Russian.

World title fights are only held in two places. Las Vegas, Nevada, or Atlantic City, New Jersey. Gaudy, glitzy monuments to mankind's passion for a punt. Plastic towns full of plastic people who sit at tables all night, playing roulette and blackjack with plastic chips.

World titles look a whole lot better, sitting watching them with a beer in your hand in a pub in Sydney.

If you're going to watch a world title fight, the pub — with a beer, a packet of peanuts, and a bar full of screaming fight fans — is the only place to be.

Yesterday, on my way to work to write a serious column about the state of the nation, I dropped into the pub to see if Kostya Tszyu and Jake 'The Snake' were in the ring. They didn't get in there for almost two hours. When the combatants finally climb into the ring, Kostya doesn't. He jumps over the top strand of the ropes, which is pretty impressive.

Jake 'The Snake' Rodriguez, defending his IBF world junior-welterweight title, is dressed in red. With matching hair. Jake is also impressive, not because he jumps over the top strand of the ropes, which he doesn't, but because he is the only Puerto Rican I have ever seen with red hair, but, as far as making an impact, that's about where it ends.

Before we can open our third pack of beer nuts, Jake is in

A welcome home from Papa after my 1989 European Championship success

Young love — Natasha and me

Standing tall after victory in the 1991 King's Cup in Bangkok. My old adversary Andreas Zuelow (beaten in the final) is on the right of the picture

Sweet success ... with coach Vladimir Chernya and the gold medal and trophies from my 1991 European Championship victory

True blue Tszyu

Me, Bill Mordey and Jeff Fenech

Preparing for my first professional fight, with trainer Johnny Lewis in 1992

KT, phone home! Johnny Lewis, Jeff Fenech and me, in Melbourne in 1992, before my first professional fight

A sign of things to come. No more Ansett Airlines. No more links with promoter Bill Mordey

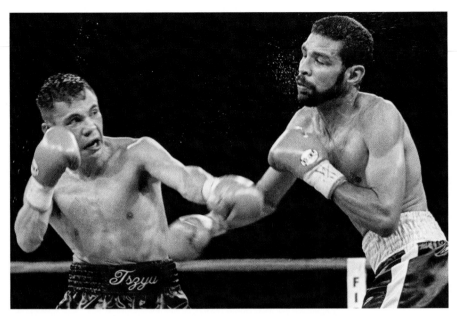

The end is nigh for Angel Hernandez in our 1994 Newcastle fight. *Ern McQuillan*

Our wedding day in Serov

At our new home at Sans Souci with son Timophey. *Ern McQuillan*

Jake Rodriguez catches me a with a right jab. But I won the fight … and the world title. *Holly Stein/Allsport*

Delighted with victory – manager/promotor Vlad Warton and me

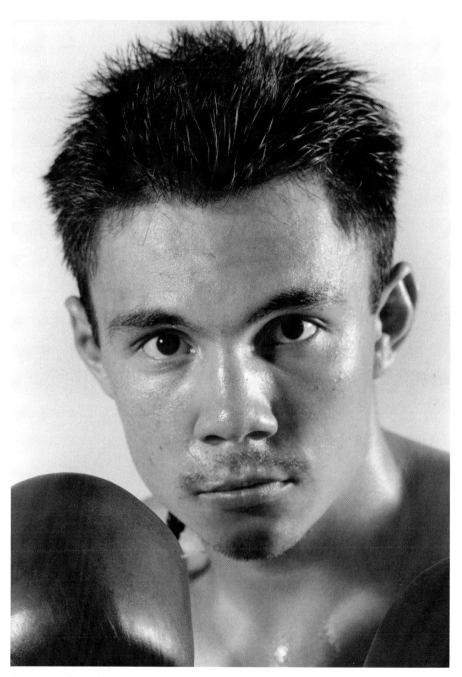

Determination wins world titles. *Ern McQuillan*

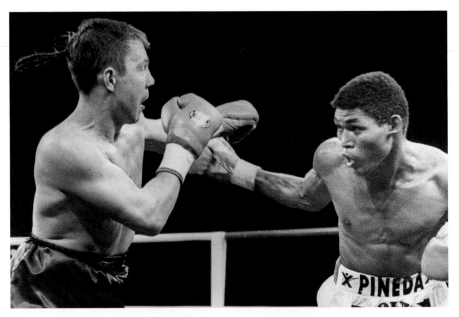

Overcoming the elements to beat Hugo Pineda at a rain-drenched Parramatta Stadium, January 1996. *Ern McQuillan*

Looking for an opening in Pineda's defences. *Ern McQuillan*

Corey Johnson misses as I head for victory in a world title defence in Sydney, 1996.
AAP Image/Rick Rycroft

Things were going well early in my 1997 fight with Vince Phillips. But he came back to inflict the only defeat of my career. *AAP Image/Allen Oliver*

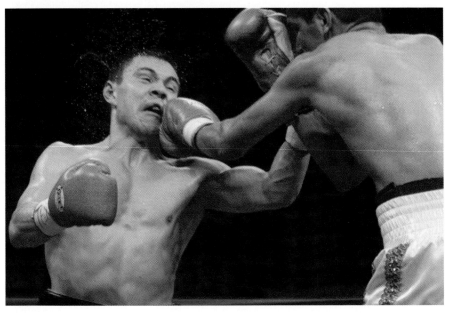

A glancing blow from Rafael Ruelas — but I finished on top in our 1998 bout at El Paso. *AAP Image/ El Paso Times/Victor Calzada*

Down and out. Referee James Jenkin about to move in and stop the fight and crown me winner against Diobelis Hurtado at Indo, California in 1998.
AAP Image/Desert Sun/Wade Byars

Miguel Angel Gonzalez takes evasive action in our 1999 Miami bout. But eventually I caught up with him for a 10th round TKO success. *AAP Image/Alan Diaz*

The spoils of victory. Ahmed Santos gave me the sombrero. I kept my WBC world title belt when I beat him in Uncasville, Connecticut in 2000. *AAP Image/Dean Lewins*

One of the greatest boxers in the history of the sport, Julio Cesar Chavez battled gamely in our bout at Phoenix, Arizona, July 2000. *AAP Image/Mike Fiala*

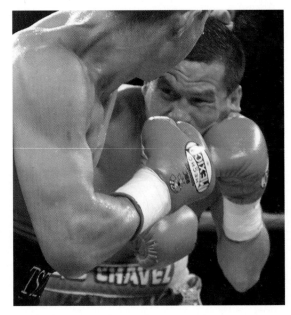

The end is nigh. Chavez tries to evade my punches. *AAP Image/Matt York*

Chavez hits the canvas. *AAP Image/Matt York*

Moments later his team threw in the towel. *AAP Image/Mike Fiala*

Sharmba Mitchell beware! These are push-ups with a difference. *AAP Image/John Gurzinski*

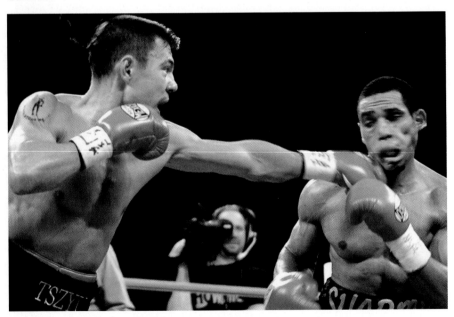

Take that! I connect with a solid left on Sharmba Mitchell. When he couldn't come out for the eighth round, I added the WBA world title to the WBC crown that was already mine. *AAP Image/John Gurzinski*

serious strife. A sweet right hand from Kostya in the opening seconds has the champ on the seat of his pants. Jake has moves. Lots of moves. More moves than Grace Bros. Unfortunately he keeps winding up at the same address. Down on the canvas at the MGM Grand. In Round Six, Jake goes down more often than the Brazilian rate of exchange.

'Finish him off, Kostya!' they scream.

A series of rights, and referee Richard Steele puts an end to Jake's agony. The Snake is gone and the Russian mongoose with the long, black pigtail and the long black pants is the new world champ.

I am glad that I stopped off at the pub on the way to work to see the fight.

This little Russian is a heck of a fighter.

Things turned sour after the fight. I threw a big party for all of the team and those like Jeff Fenech who had come to support me. One person was missing, Bill Mordey. He was angry about Vlad's involvement, especially as Vlad wanted my contract rewritten. I wanted Bill to be there to share our excitement, but he was downstairs in a bar with a glass of bourbon drinking by himself.

At the end of the evening I discovered that all my jewellery had been stolen from my hotel room. There was around $7000 worth of watches, rings and chains. I thought that someone who had come to the party had stolen them. What else could I think? But I was to find out the next day that the hotel video surveillance had caught a fellow breaking into the room while I was at the fight. He tried twice. The first time he aborted his attempt to get into the room because a cleaner appeared. The next time he succeeded. Even though he was caught on video the culprit was never identified. When I checked with Bill about insurance, I discovered he hadn't taken out a policy to cover such things, and he became angry when I questioned him about it.

I discovered an envelope he had handed me when we left

Sydney. I hadn't thought anything about it and tossed it in my suitcase to look at it later. However, now, as I was going through my belongings to see what had been stolen, I noticed the envelope. In it was a legal letter saying he was taking up the option of another two years on my contract. Enclosed was a cheque for one dollar as payment for the option.

Mutual trust had disappeared. Little irritations had been building up from the time Bill didn't want me to go on a holiday with my family two years before. The one dollar cheque was the straw that broke the camel's back. I decided there and then that my relationship with Bill Mordey was over. I'd make it official when I returned to Sydney.

I arrived home to see the headlines on the front page of our local newspaper, the *St George Leader* — 'Surprise awaiting champion Kostya'. What could be the surprise? The story said that Natasha wanted another baby. 'I'd like to plan for the future,' she was reported as saying. Timophey was not yet three months old but she was already thinking about another child. One thing in the story was certain however. Natasha was determined not to miss my future fights. I had run up a huge phone bill, calling every day to see how she was and how Timophey was progressing. He had started to sit up by himself for the first time. That was a real milestone in his life — as I had just reached a milestone in mine.

Just over a month later, on 19 May 1995, Natasha and I joined Timophey as Australian citizens. At a quiet ceremony at Rockdale Town Hall we (and half a dozen other 'new Australians') were given this great honour. As I was to tell a group of newcomers at Adelaide Town Hall five years later, when I was guest of honour at a similar ceremony, this country is the best in the world. I'm someone who has travelled to many, many countries during my career. I've never seen a better country in which to live and bring up our children.

Back in Australia I made the split with Mordey official. Bill threatened to sue and he eventually did. From then on Vlad would be both my manager and promoter. Vlad told the press, 'I didn't ask for the job. It's just a matter of there being no one else around. People say the American promoters won't accept me. Well, they'll just have to. Kostya is the world champion and I'm his manager and promoter. End of story. And bullying won't work. I'm used to that from my days as a young kid who couldn't speak English standing up to those who poked fun at me.'

Meanwhile Bill's friends in the media published his rhetoric, suggesting that I had stabbed him in the back. Most of the journalists didn't want to hear my side of the story. It looked as if I would just have to prove myself in the ring all over again.

THE BLACK MAMBA

I have never known an athlete in any chosen sport, anywhere in the world, who is more focused than Kostya in what he is trying to achieve.
— Johnny Lewis

My first world title defence was to be back in Australia in June 1995. I had been offered big money to fight in America, but preferred to be on home territory, back at the Newcastle Entertainment Centre, which now seemed like my second home.

It was to be extra special as it was the first time I had fought since becoming an Australian citizen. My American opponent would be no pushover. Roger Mayweather had been dubbed 'The Black Mamba' because his aggressive nature reminded people of the venomous African snake. He had, in his 14-year professional career, won two major world titles, losing them both to one of the greats of the sport, Julio Cesar Chavez. When Mayweather came to Australia he still held a minor world welterweight crown recognised by the little-known International Boxing Organisation (IBO).

Kostya has so much going for him. His punches are explosive. He has an incredible hand speed. He knows no fear and he has an abundance of natural talent, but what sets him apart from all the other thousands of would-be champions is his mental approach. I have never known an athlete in any chosen sport, anywhere in the world, who is more focused than Kostya in what he is trying to achieve. The mental side to Kostya is just unbelievable. I suppose it probably has a lot to do with his background and the fact that he had so many amateur fights. It has all been regimented in his mind. He has an amazing ability to become focused on the immediate job on hand. He leaves absolutely nothing to chance.

He was asked by a television bloke the other day about the fact that bookmakers had him a hot favourite to win the world title in Las Vegas. Kostya's reply was a simple 'So what?' He knows that public perceptions don't mean a thing when he steps into the ring. Lots of good fighters have won titles, but then they have lost the necessary ingredients that helped get them there in the first place. They got beaten taking shortcuts.

Kostya realises this. He wants to be recognised as the greatest junior-welterweight of all time. He has the potential to be great, and he will do absolutely everything to achieve that goal.
— *Johnny Lewis, speaking at a media conference in Newcastle before the Mayweather fight*

Johnny understood my mental approach to boxing. He was also right about another thing — I was determined to become the greatest junior-welterweight, maybe not of all time, but most definitely of my era.

Mayweather certainly gave me a good fight, taking me the full 12 rounds, and he left me with plenty of cuts and bruises, the results of many head clashes. My left ear was badly swollen and there was a gash in the corner of my left eye, the latter opened up in the ninth round and again late in the last. Mayweather used spoiling tactics to stop me from landing my heaviest rights. But, although I couldn't put him away for the count, I posted an easy points victory. The American judge Paul Weitzel had me ahead 119 points to 109. The Aussie Charlie Lucas and Filipino Pascual Ingusan had it fractionally closer, with me winning 118-110. It was a really good workout for my next fight, a mandatory title defence.

ROGER MAYWEATHER (USA)

World title fights
WBA super-featherweight

19 January 1983	W TKO8	Samuel Serrano at San Juan, Puerto Rico
20 April 1983	W TKO8	Jorge Alvarado at San Jose, USA
17 August 1983	W KO1	Benedicto Villablanca at Las Vegas, USA
27 February 1984	L KO1	Rocky Lockridge at Beaumont, USA
7 July 1985	L KO2	Julio Cesar Chavez at Las Vegas, USA

WBC junior-welterweight

12 November 1987	W TKO6	Rene Arredondo at Inglewood, USA
4 March 1988	W KO3	Mauricio Aceves at Los Angeles, USA
6 June 1988	W TKO12	Rodolfo Gonzalez at Los Angeles, USA
7 November 1988	W Pts12	Vinnie Pazienza at Las Vegas, USA
13 May 1989	L TKO10	Julio Cesar Chavez at Inglewood, USA

IBF junior-welterweight

| 7 December 1991 | L KO9 | Rafael Pineda at Reno, USA |

IBO welterweight

27 May 1994	W KO3	Eduardo Montes at St George, USA
4 August 1994	W Pts12	Johnny Bizzarro at Ledyard, USA
17 February 1995	W TKO9	Aaron McLaurine at Las Vegas, USA

WET AND WILD

The first challenge to my world crown had been successfully repelled and I prepared for the mandatory challenge from Colombian Hugo Pineda. I thought everything would be straightforward. How wrong I was. These compulsory defences are offered to the highest bidder. Every promoter that is interested sends a bid in a sealed envelope to the governing body, in this case the IBF, who are then supposed to open the envelopes at a public ceremony. The highest bidder gets to promote the fight. Vlad reckoned his bid of several million would be the best on offer. Imagine our surprise when the envelopes were opened and Pineda's own promoter Billy Chams had made an almost identical bid in all aspects but with an offer that was $US900 more than Vlad's.

Chams told us he would be staging the fight in Colombia. It was not the most stable of countries at the best of times what with fights between drug barons and riots among factions opposed to the government. Indeed, at that time, a state of emergency had been declared and the country was under martial law. We feared for our lives if we went there. When we refused to fight there the IBF stripped me of my title. The IBF officials said they had checked with the US State Department and, according to the advice the US government was giving tourists, the situation in two of the cities in Colombia, where big fights were usually staged, the Caribbean ports of Cartagena and Barranquilla (Pineda's birthplace), was 'not too bad'. Not too bad? What sort of guarantee was that?

I was upset enough, but things became even worse when Bill Mordey went public to declare such a thing would never have happened if he had still been running the show. 'That's what happens when the monkeys get out of the cage and try to run the zoo.'

We were undeterred. Vlad took the IBF to court in the United States and won. I got to keep my title and, after buying the rights from Chams, Vlad got to promote the fight in Australia. I had insisted on that. The decision probably cost me around $750,000. If I had agreed to have the fight in Colombia I would have made a lot more money, but I owed it to the people of Australia. After all, Australia had offered me a new home, a new life and a new nationality. It was the least I could do in return, and I felt much more comfortable fighting here. I had also been told that only an early knockout would have ensured I retained my title in a Colombian arena.

The fight was set down for Parramatta Stadium in Sydney's west on Saturday, 20 January 1996. Pineda was a dangerous opponent. He was unbeaten in his latest 17 fights. One of these was a controversial draw with fellow countryman Bernardos Contreras in Cartagena in March four years earlier. He had wiped the slate with an eight-round points win over Contreras two months later. Twenty of Pineda's 26 victories during his career had been inside the distance including three first-round knockouts and seven others in the second round. He had won the Latin-American title two years before and had successfully defended this title three times. I was leaving nothing to chance and enlisted the aid of Hector Lopez, the fellow who had almost beaten me in Tampa, Florida, three fights before my world championship success. I flew him across the Pacific to be my main sparring partner and he would take on one of Pineda's troupe, Ener Julio, on the undercard.

At the weigh-in at the Rooty Hill RSL Club the day before the fight I weighed in 10 grams heavier than Pineda, who was cocky about his chances.

'I have seen seven videotapes of Tszyu's fights,' he said with a dismissive shake of the head. 'I don't see a single problem. Tomorrow, I'm going to be the new world champion.' His trainer, Amilcar Brusa, had all the right credentials. He had shaped the career of Carlos Monzon, one of the greatest fighters in the history of our sport. Brusa also dismissed my chances of victory.

'Tszyu is very good in attack,' he told the assembled media. 'In defence he is not so good.'

I had news for him. So, too, did Johnny Lewis and Jeff Fenech. 'Kostya will have to improve at least 50 per cent on his last fight effort against Roger Mayweather to beat this kid,' Johnny said. 'But he most certainly will. You should see some of the body shots he has been putting in during his sparring sessions. They have been dynamite, pure dynamite.' Fenech noticed Pineda's build. One journalist said he was so skinny that he looked like a praying mantis when he shaped up in the ring.

'A guy that tall and skinny has to be fragile,' Fenech pointed out.

Problems with the promotion started before the bout took place. When we picked the date, we hadn't realised that the World Series Cricket final was to be shown live on free-to-air television that same night. Many sporting fans would be tempted to stay at home and watch the cricket instead of paying money to watch me fight. Then there was a fire brigade strike at Rome Airport that resulted in the official IBF supervisor, Benedetto Montella, missing not only the lead-up to the big night but the fight itself. And before Vlad had got the contract to stage the bout in Sydney from Chams, the Colombian had sold the Australian television rights for the fight to Premier All Star Sports, a rival to Sky Channel to which I was contracted. Premier decided to show the fight live in theatres and clubs near Parramatta Stadium in direct competition to us.

Then around 6pm a thunderstorm hit the stadium. As lightning cracked and thunder boomed fans tried to cram under what little cover there was. Meanwhile Chams had announced Pineda would not be fighting unless he saw the colour of Vlad's money. Chams claimed the IBF president had told him Pineda was not to step into the ring unless the IBF's fee for sanctioning the bout had been paid 'in cash'. This was unusual — as the fee was usually sent off to the ruling body by cheque after the fight. Where was Vlad supposed to get tens of thousands of dollars in cash on a Saturday evening? Eventually Chams was placated, and after the water was swept from the ring, the preliminaries got underway. My sparring partner Lopez beat Julio on points over 10 rounds, which was a good omen for me.

There were around 11,000 wet but excited fans to cheer me on once Pineda and I finally made it into the ring. In the first round Pineda caught me off guard with a clever right hand. It was more of a slip than a knockdown and I winked at Johnny to let him know I was okay. Actually the mishap was good for me. It ensured I didn't underestimate Pineda. A sort of early wake-up call. Pineda hit me with a number of low blows. A couple were so blatant that referee Billy Males twice ordered points be deducted from the Colombian's tally. At one stage he went to Pineda's corner to tell them he had had enough of the persistent fouls. I hammered Pineda with solid rights that knocked him to the canvas in both the fourth and seventh rounds. The further the bout went the further I went in front. Pineda was a really game fighter and refused to give up. When I knocked him down three times in the 11th round, the referee finally stepped in and stopped the fight.

Johnny told reporters, 'You'd have to go a long way to see a better fight than that. They were both great fighters. It is just that Kostya is in a class of his own. Some of his right hands would have stopped a buffalo. It's amazing how Pineda survived as long as he did.'

South African Jan Piet Bergman, the No. 2 contender, was ringside. He knew my next mandatory defence would almost certainly be against him and he had flown out to see me in action first hand. He refused to be drawn into comment. 'It was an interesting fight,' was all he would say.

HUGO PINEDA (Colombia)		
Title fights		
Latin American light-welterweight		
25 March 1994	W Pts12	Jose Barboza at Barranquilla, Colombia
18 June 1994	W TKO6	Jose Maria Escobar at Buenos Aires, Argentina
3 December 1994	W TKO11	Pedro Padilla Estrada at Bogota, Colombia
20 May 1995	W TKO2	Faustino Barrios at Buenos Aires, Argentina

For a long while I had to put up with bad-mouthing from Shannan Taylor, a more-than-competent fighter from Wollongong. He had been stalking me, suggesting that I was afraid to fight him. Nothing could have been further from the truth. There was just no point in fighting him. He didn't have the necessary credentials. I had easily beaten him in our only fight as an amateur, in an insignificant tournament in the Philippines. He had finished nowhere in the world amateur championships in Sydney, at which I had collected the gold medal. He made his professional debut four months after me and fought the same boxer first up, knocking out Darrell Hiles in the second round of their fight in Taylor's hometown of Wollongong.

Taylor and I had been involved in a spar at the Newtown gym in 1994 and Taylor had taken it all too seriously. The famous ring commentator Ray Connelly was there at the time and before he died he described the situation: 'In the second round they were on the ropes and Shannan pushed his shoulder up under Kostya's chin. He didn't respond straightaway, but in the next round, in virtually the same spot, he did it again. This time Kostya unleashed a fearsome combination of punches. Kostya said [after the confrontation], "the next time I spar him, I kill him".' Shannon was a silly boy and lucky it wasn't a real fight, otherwise he would have got a real hammering.

Now Shannan Taylor was Bill Mordey's great hope for a world championship, but in reality he was just not good enough to beat any of the champions. He fought Livingstone Bramble at Toowoomba in November 1995. When he won, with a first-round knockout, his team went around boasting about what he had done and how I hadn't been able to knock Bramble out in the 10 rounds of our fight. What they failed to mention was that Bramble had never been quite the same fighter after I beat him and had lost the three bouts before he shaped up to Taylor.

To shut up Taylor and his entourage Vlad chose, as my next opponent, the same boxer who had fought a controversial draw with Taylor in Dublin two months earlier, American Corey Johnson. The Detroit fighter had lost only one bout in his career, to a fine boxer, Stevie Johnston, who would later win the WBC world lightweight title. While it was officially a draw, in the Dublin fight Johnson had put Taylor down on his backside in a display that should have given him victory. I would prove to the Taylor camp how to handle Johnson.

Some 9000 fans were at the Sydney Entertainment Centre on the night of 24 May 1996 to see me put Johnson away in four rounds. He thought I would go for his head so he kept his defences high. Instead, I attacked his body and eventually he could not take it any more. Don't get me wrong; Johnson was a great boxer. In a dozen or so fights after our bout, from America to Wales and Denmark, he was unbeaten while never breaking through for another title challenge. I was to eventually use him as a sparring partner in preparation for later bouts because of his ability.

24
NOT JUST A PALOOKA

We always thought Kostya was great. Now we know more.
Mr Tszyu, you're the man.
— former US Olympic team trainer Ken Adams

My next bout was a mandatory defence of my IBF junior-welterweight title against the No. 1 contender, South African champion Jan Piet Bergman, back in Newcastle on 14 September 1996. It would not be easy. Bergman had won the WBC International Junior-welterweight Championship three years earlier in Sun City, South Africa. He had an impressive unbeaten record with 24 of his 32 successes by knockout.

I knew Bergman was a good fighter. I had met him a few times outside the ring and he was a likeable bloke. However, I wouldn't be talking to him before the fight. That would not be good for my mental preparation. I told the media that he would give me a good fight because he was a tall, strong boxer, but when you are fighting the top contenders, everyone is strong. I had the world championship belt, but to keep it I must fight the best, and to beat the best I must improve with every fight, become stronger with every fight. I would beat Bergman, and when the fight was over we could become friends again.

Johnny Lewis was confident, too. 'Bergman can box but Kostya's powerful punch is his ace card, the trump card. Bergman isn't as strong as Kostya. Quite frankly, at his weight, I don't think anyone in the world is anywhere near as strong. Kostya just keeps improving, doing things I've never seen any other boxer do. He's a freak.'

I was taking nothing for granted. I had a lot of respect for Bergman's ability, so I pushed myself to the limit in training. I knew he was good and that I had to be that much better.

The fight went according to plan. I stalked Bergman for the first few rounds piling up points with my jabs and combinations. Jab, jab, jab. He did not know how to counter, and when my right went into action he could not counter. In the second round I opened a cut on his face and he seemed to lose his cool and started to throw wild punches. This just played into my hands.

In the sixth round there was a clash of heads, an accidental headbutt from Bergman, for which neither of us were to blame. A gaping wound opened under my left eye. It didn't worry me, but the referee, Billy Males, stopped the fight for a moment to allow the fight medical officer, Dr Lou Lewis, to examine the cut. I knew the doctor would let the fight continue. Just to make sure about the result, when the referee called 'fight on' I knew I should step up my attack. I went for broke. I hit Bergman with a great right combination. He hit the ropes and slid to the canvas. He was up and ready to fight at the count of eight, but I could see he was not prepared for the next onslaught. I hit him with a right hook, a telling left cross and finally with a solid straight right. He hit the deck and slid under the ropes and into a television monitor. It was all over in 1 minute 26 seconds into the sixth round. The referee, Billy Males, later explained: 'Kostya hit him so hard, Bergman was unconscious before he was halfway to the floor.'

Papa and Johnny were quickly into the ring to embrace me. As usual I felt very, very proud. I grabbed the microphone to talk to the 6000 fans who were chanting 'Tszyu, Tszyu, Tszyu!'

'Hello, Newcastle. This was one of my best fights. When I won the world title I knew I had to fight anyone — the best. That's why I am still the world champion because I keep fighting the best fighters at my weight. I am prepared to fight anyone in my weight division at the right time for the right money.'

An indication as to what a good fight it had been was shown in the scorecards of the three judges. When the bout was stopped both Australian judge Ray Wheatley and South African judge Stanley Christodolou had me in front 48-47 while the neutral official, American Pete Podgorski, had me leading 49-46.

Here's how others saw my fight:

You can't take anything away from Kostya. I gave my best. I tried to neutralise the fight when I felt the trickle of blood in my eye, but he was too good. Kostya showed me my mistakes and I'll have to work hard to eliminate them in the future.
— *Jan Piet Bergman, very gracious in defeat*

We always thought Kostya was great. Now we know more. Mr Tszyu, you're the man. Kostya is explosive. He taught Jan a lot of lessons.
— *one of the Bergman team, the former US Olympic team trainer Ken Adams*

I though my man [Bergman] could win. I know the boxing game very well and Jan wasn't just some Palooka without a chance. He was a legitimate No. 1 contender and the former WBC International champion, but I was truly overwhelmed by the way Kostya won in such an impressive fashion. I think he is a great, great champion. The world, not only Australia, will see and hear a lot more about this young man in the future.
— *Cedric Kushner, South African boxing promoter and television entrepreneur*

A great fighter beat a good fighter. Bergman will learn more from this loss than he has from any of his previous fights. If he fights for another 10 years, he won't fight anyone better than Kostya. Everyone underestimates Kostya's power. They watch videos, but videos don't measure his real power.
— *Johnny Lewis*

After the fight we headed back to the Newcastle Wests Leagues Club to celebrate. It was a double celebration. Not only had I kept my title — but it was also the birthday of my masseur and great friend Roman Lubouny. More than a little vodka was consumed that night.

JAN PIET BERGMAN (South Africa)	
World title fights	
WBC International light-welterweight	
26 June 1993	W TKO10 Viktor Baranov at Sun City, South Africa
6 October 1993	W TKO7 Kamel Bou Ali at Johannesburg, South Africa
20 November 1993	W KO5 Jesus Rojas at Johannesburg, South Africa
18 April 1995	W Pts12 Ray Collins at Las Vegas, USA

This was the last time I was able to defend a world title in New-castle, my 'home-away-from-home'. Respected *Newcastle Herald* columnist Stewart Roach explained the effect my regular visits to the steel city had on the local population:

The melodic alliterate introductions by ring announcer Ray Connelly at the Newcastle Entertainment Centre may have claimed Kostya Tszyu was from Sydney, but he was just as much at home in Newcastle as he was in Sans Souci.

The steel city was his second home in Australia.

When in Newcastle he would regularly visit such places as the BHP steelworks, the Alcan aluminium plant and Stockton Hospital where he always received a hero's welcome. His public appearances were many and varied. They included a visit to Broadmeadow Racecourse where a horse was named in his honour — although it never quite reached the dizzy heights of its namesake.

Tszyu trained at the local Broadmeadow Youth Club in sessions open to the public, and every time he walked through the foyer of the Wests Leagues Club, adjacent to where he was staying, he would be greeted by a rousing round of applause. He often stayed signing autographs long after Johnny Lewis and Bill Mordey had retired for the evening. He also endeared himself to the locals by suggesting that the smokestacks so characteristic of Newcastle's industry reminded him of his home city of Serov.

Tszyu's introduction to the working class crowd at Newcastle Entertainment Centre was brief. He quickly won their hearts with his trademark entrance, vaulting over the top ring rope. The introductory fanfare and anthems took about 8 minutes, but Tszyu needed only 2 minutes and 42 seconds to lay American Larry LaCoursiere cold on the canvas. The 3500 loved it. They were delirious, shouting the house down.

A month later they were back in force, bringing more mates with them, and Kostya reacted to their shouts of support by flooring American Robert Rivera after 40 seconds and finishing him off with a vicious right to the jaw in the 87th second.

Tszyu visited the BHP steelworks before he took on former WBA world champion Livingstone Bramble in his next Newcastle fight. The BHP riggers made a mock coffin for poor old Livingstone, and they all taped imitation rats' tails to the back of their safety helmets in Kostya's honour.

He went the distance with Bramble and when he won, the Newcastle fans screamed for a future world title fight in the city. Such was his popularity that when he beat Angel Hernandez in a seventh-round TKO in May 1994, local radio station 2HD broadcast the fight to listeners in the Hunter Valley. It was the first fight broadcast on local radio in 40 years.

The Newcastle fans got their world title clash — Tszyu's first defence of his new crown, against Roger Mayweather in the following June. It was also his first fight as a 'dinki-di' Aussie after he and wife Natasha had gained their Australian citizenship. Later that year, he expressed his feelings about the Novocastrians. Just before he demolished South African Jan Bergman he explained why he loved fighting in the steel city: 'It's the atmosphere in Newcastle before a fight. I've never had anything like it elsewhere. I love the support the people of Newcastle have given me.'

The people of Newcastle have also loved the support he has given them.

GIVE US BACK OUR PANTS

Kostya's a beast. In the ring he comes at you like an
animal on the prowl wanting to savage you.
— Oscar de la Hoya, WBC junior-welterweight champion

Johnny Lewis did not have fond memories of Las Vegas. It was there on 28 June 1991 that he had watched from the corner as Jeff Fenech had out-boxed, out-punched and outwitted Azumah Nelson in their WBC super-featherweight world championship bout, only to see the judges rule a draw.

So you can see why Johnny never felt at ease in the Nevada gambling metropolis. It seemed like a case of déjà vu when we went there in January 1997 for the fourth defence of my IBF world crown, against Puerto Rican Leonardo Mas. Joe Cortez, the same referee who had controlled the Fenech-Nelson clash, would be in charge of my bout.

It was my first time back in Las Vegas since winning the title from 'Jake the Snake'. This time I made sure all my valuables were under lock and key when I fought, just in case another robber came calling while I was busy disposing of Mas.

The Puerto Rican was a mysterious fellow, whose record showed him unbeaten. We weren't sure if there were some fights that didn't appear on his CV. We weren't even sure exactly how old he was. He had won the Caribbean welterweight title a couple of years earlier and in his most recent bout, three months before we shaped up to each other, he had beaten Mexican Javier 'Changa' Marquez on a technicality to take the Central American junior-welterweight crown. A technicality? We were soon to realise the significance of that.

Promoter Bob Arum had arranged our fight to be on the under-card of a major bout involving American Oscar de la Hoya and Mexican Miguel Angel Gonzales, a bloke I was destined to meet a couple of years later. De la Hoya was the 'darling' of the American boxing scene. He had won the 1982 Olympic title and on the victory dais had carried both the American and Mexican flags (the latter in honour of his late mother who had been born in Mexico). He had gone go on to win the WBO super-featherweight, the IBF and WBO world lightweight and the WBC junior-welterweight world crowns. In his previous fight de la Hoya had won the WBC title from Julio Cesar Chavez, another fellow I was to fight at a future date.

Arum had it in mind to have Oscar fighting me some time down the track. That's why he had me fight on the same evening. 'One day these two — Oscar and Kostya — will be matched in boxing's "Super Fight",' he said at the weigh-in, and the media played along with Arum. They even claimed to have me telling Oscar before our respective bouts, 'I want to fight you. I want what you've got [the WBC crown].' Anyone who knows me realised that wasn't my style, even if I would have liked to have had the WBC title as well as the

IBF crown. The press also had Oscar saying, 'Kostya Tszyu is a great world champion. He's a beast. In the ring he comes at you like an animal on the prowl wanting to savage you.' It was all good publicity.

We've never met. Oscar later went up a couple of weight divisions, and achieved the outstanding record of winning world titles in five different weight categories.

Oscar had a good win that evening in Las Vegas. My bout was quite controversial and left a bitter taste in my mouth. It was one of the most one-sided fights of my career. I knocked Mas to the canvas after 35 seconds. He staggered to his feet and tried to get away from me, but it was to no avail. I caught him and sent him to the canvas for a second time, then a third. There was just 25 seconds of the round remaining. I had caught him on the jaw and was sure I had broken it because it was hanging at an unusual angle while he propped himself up on one knee. The referee halted the fight and called a doctor into the ring. The doctor looked at Mas and shook his head.

But as I waited for Cortez to raise my hand in triumph he shocked us all. He declared the fight a technical draw. Cortez claimed I had hit Mas with an unintentional foul blow, saying he had called on us to break a clinch and I had obviously not heard him before I landed the last deadly punch. My perfect record was blemished. Okay, so I still held the title, but there it was in black and white — 18-0-1 (18 wins, no losses and a draw) instead of 19-0-0. Everyone except Mas and his team were dumbfounded. Ringside judge Robert Holmes told the press he never heard Cortez call 'break'. Rich Moranda, who was calling the fight on HBO cable television, re-ran the video of the finish over and over again and shook his head in disbelief, 'It's kinda hard to see any illegal blow.'

Johnny was furious. Newspaper reports quoted him as saying, 'I don't mind if you screw us every time we come to this town, but please give us our pants back afterwards.' I'm not sure whether he really made this comment. But I know he was very, very angry. Vlad threatened to take the IBF to court again. He said he would appeal to the Nevada State Boxing Commission to have the decision changed to a TKO, but he soon calmed down and realised that would only be throwing good money after bad.

When I arrived home 48 hours later, the Aussie journalists were at Sydney Airport to greet me and all they wanted to talk about was the controversial decision.

'I think the referee was shaken and confused and did not know what to do,' I told them. 'I will write a nice letter of appeal today to the IBF. I am a clean fighter. I didn't make an illegal punch, and I won easily. You all saw it on the television.' And I added a comment I hoped would get back to the boxing chiefs, 'I am proud to be the IBF champion. I know they are fair and I hope they will help me by restoring my perfect record.'

Johnny was outspoken. He told the reporters: 'Kostya's final punch would have dropped an elephant. Maybe Cortez's action was just a case of one Puerto Rican looking after another.'

Jeff Fenech's memories of the Azumah Nelson decision came to the fore when the media questioned him. 'Typical Vegas shit!' he said. 'I honestly think Cortez is incompetent. He just loves to get his melon [head] on TV.' And then Jeff added a rider: 'I was never able to come back after my Las Vegas disappointment, but Kostya most certainly will.'

What happened in Las Vegas would soon pale into insignificance. Bill Mordey had been true to his word and had begun court action against me. Little did I know what a traumatic outcome it would be.

The court fight with Bill Mordey was like a nightmare. Bill had been like a big brother to me since I had come to Australia. He had been part of my 'family', but it had, without warning, fallen apart.

Bill was suing me and my company Tszyu Enterprises, Vlad Warton, Jeff Fenech, businessman Theo Onisforou (who had dealt with Vlad), and Sky Channel.

Bill claimed I had broken my contract with him after winning the world title, and the others had induced me to take that action. The sticking point was that Mordey's company had a deal with Foxtel to show my fights. We had a deal with Sky Channel.

Mordey was demanding $10 million in damages. My lawyers were arguing that the contract was unconscionable — a legal word that meant it was so fragile and unfair as to be invalid. They also suggested that even if the contract was valid, the damages he was demanding were preposterous, way out of proportion to what I could have earned for Mordey had I still been in his camp.

The timing of the court case could not have been worse. It opened in Court 11C at the NSW Supreme Court in Sydney on 24 March 1997. I was due to defend my world title against Vince Phillips in Atlantic City eight weeks later. I should have been in full training. Instead I was in court for a hearing before Justice Bainton. My mind should have been focused exclusively on Phillips. Instead I was worrying about what would happen if I should lose the case. My lawyers had told me it was clear cut and I would definitely come out on top, but I had seen so many certainties beaten in the ring, I was still wary.

When I appeared in court on the third day of the hearing, I tried to explain just why I had split with Bill, and that it was not about money as Bill tried to make out. No, it was about the little things in life. As I told Justice Bainton there was my disappointment at Bill not offering me congratulations and not joining in my victory party after the world title success over Jake Rodriguez. There was also the fact that he had signed an agreement with a company producing swap cards without my knowledge. The first thing I knew about them was when someone asked me to sign one in Las Vegas. 'How could he do this?' I asked the court. 'Many people may find such things trivial. Yes, small things, but so many small things. It's like a glass of water. If you put too much water in the glass it will overflow. The same thing happened to me.'

At one stage in the court proceedings it was suggested I had earned $900,000 in the three years I had fought for Mordey. I had to interject that after tax, expenses and paying Johnny Lewis his 25 per cent the figure was nearer $300,000. The judge, however, didn't want to know about such things. He made it clear he was there to decide whether my contract with Bill was valid. My time in the witness box was a nightmare. My English was still very shaky. I did not understand a lot of what was being said, especially the legal language used by the barristers. Much was made of which of Mordey's companies paid the cheques to me. His former company Classic Promotions or his later company Fightvision. This was apparently crucial to the legal argument. I told the court I didn't pay much attention to what name was on each cheque, I just put them in the bank.

I was asked if I thought I could beat Frankie Randall, Julio Cesar Chavez, Oscar de la Hoya and Pernell Whittaker, the top fighters in my weight division, another crucial point in the legal jousting. I answered truthfully by saying I could, although not in one go. Evidence was given that a fight between Chavez and de la Hoya had grossed $19 million. Mordey claimed I should have been de la Hoya's opponent, and he and I should have been getting a share of that money.

After each day in court, I would rush off to Newtown and try to focus on my training. Every day the hearing continued was a bonus to Vince Phillips.

The summing up by the barristers took several days and after 13 days in the Supreme Court the hearing was over. It was left to Justice Bainton to decide. Was it a case of greed by me, and my advisers, as Mordey claimed? Or was it a series of personal and professional mistakes by Mordey that led to my losing my trust for him and looking elsewhere for a better deal? The judge would not make his decision for almost a year, leaving me to worry about the outcome.

26

COOL AS A CUCUMBER

*His eyes ... were full of tears, but his pride would not
let him shed even one single tear. Not one!*
— Natasha

Members of the media continued to talk up the possibility of a
fight between me and the pin-up of world boxing Oscar de
la Hoya. It would have been a promoter's dream. De la Hoya had
won gold at the Barcelona Olympics at the time I was fighting
LaPorte in Sydney in my fourth professional bout. Our careers had
run almost parallel, me in Russia and he in the United States.
He had started boxing at the age of seven, and when I won the
junior-welterweight gold at the Goodwill Games he took gold in the
light-weight division, but he had surprisingly lost his first bout in
the world championships at Sydney, where I had won gold in my
division.

As a professional, de la Hoya was now unbeaten in 27 fights. Twenty-two of those fights had been won by knockout, and he had won five different versions of the world championship in three different weight divisions from junior-lightweight to welterweight, of which he was then the WBC champ. Although he was a weight division above me, there was talk that he would strip down to meet me halfway. Vlad would always tell reporters, 'The fight won't happen. De la Hoya's people are worried about the power in Kostya's punches.' Aside from this we were also in different Pay TV camps — and neither network was likely to give away one of their box office stars to the other.

Meanwhile, I had accepted a challenge from the tough, 33-year-old veteran American Vince 'Cool' Phillips. He was a big fellow who normally fought as a welterweight and had to shed a lot of poundage to make the limit, but I knew there was mental toughness there. He was a former drug addict whose self-will had helped him kick the habit. In his twenties Phillips had got stuck into booze and marijuana before graduating to cocaine. Although he had a good fighting record the drugs looked likely to bring about his downfall. Twice he had tested positive to drugs — the first time to pot, the second to coke. At the time the boxing authorities had taken away his world rankings and his future looked bleak, but he pulled himself together. A few weeks before our fight he had celebrated his fourth year free of drugs and alcohol.

The previous year Phillips had earned a shot at the WBA world welterweight title, but had been hammered into submission in the third round by the unbeaten champion Ike 'Bazooka' Quartey from Ghana. It was no disgrace. Quartey held the title for five years until he was eventually beaten by de la Hoya in 1999. Phillips had lost his most recent bout — a points decision over 10 rounds to a solid, if unspectacular, American light-middleweight named Romallis Ellis.

The bookmakers had Phillips as a 20-1 outsider in our upcoming fight. They were ridiculous odds in a 'two-horse' race. Johnny warned me not to underestimate this cagey American. He hadn't wanted Vlad to put Phillips in the ring with me, claiming the American's style of standing up and taking punishment before launching his own assault could prove a real problem. We were also at odds about certain minor aspects of my preparation.

The fight was set for 31 May 1997 at the Taj Mahal Casino in Atlantic City, New Jersey, another of those gaudy American gambling palaces that use world title fights to help attract the punters and help relieve them of their money. There was the usual pre-fight dirty tactics. Phillips' team kept implying that I was taking performance-enhancing drugs and demanded I take a drug test. This was rich coming from a camp whose fighter was a self-confessed drug addict. These childish antics did not concern me, but the worry about the court case did. For the first time in my career I was not focused on the task ahead. As I tried to sleep at nights I would be thinking about what had happened between Bill and me, rather than thinking about how I was going to beat Vince Phillips.

The fight itself started according to plan. I was on the attack in the early rounds scoring points with clever combinations of punches. Phillips was content to go on the back foot and rely on trying to counter-punch his way into the fight, but I thought that because he had shed so much weight to drop back a division to fight me, the fasting he had undergone would eventually tell against him as the fight progressed. My jabs were taking effect, and halfway through the fight he was bleeding badly from the mouth. I kept it up. Jab, jab, jab. Then the rights, bang, bang, bang. I found out later that by the seventh round I was a clear leader. There were two American judges (Melvina Lathon and Debra Barnes) and they each had me well in front by four points. The Aussie judge Des Bloyd had us even on points.

I can honestly say that until the Phillips fight I had never felt pain during a fight. Of course, many times I had felt tired, but that was an entirely different kettle of fish. Suddenly in the Phillips fight I began to experience this strange feeling — pain. It was all new to me. Punches I would normally ignore felt like blows from a sledgehammer. They hurt, and my head refused to react because of the pain. In the seventh round, a right from Phillips to my left eye knocked me to the canvas. It was only the second time in my career such a thing had happened. His punches were hurting and I did not know how to counter. My mental toughness had disappeared. In the ninth I caught him with a solid blow and a huge split opened beside his right eye. During the break between rounds his team apparently had trouble stemming the flow of blood, but Phillips demanded to continue. Soon after the start of Round 10 referee Benjie Esteves called the official fight doctor into the ring to examine Phillips' eye and to see if the bout should be stopped. Had he done so I would have retained my world title because Lathon had me ahead on points, Bloyd favoured Phillips and Barnes had us even. A split decision and I would still have been champ. The doctor said Phillips could continue and he knew he must act quickly. He caught me with a straight right. It hurt. I dropped my guard and Phillips came in with a flurry of rights that had me reeling. My legs wouldn't obey me as I staggered backwards. My fists wouldn't move. I was feeling incredible pain. Twenty seconds before the end of Round 10, the referee moved in and stopped the fight.

Johnny told me later he was within seconds of throwing in the towel to stop me from taking any more punishment. I was angry. 'Don't ever do that, Johnny,' I protested. 'Don't ever give up on me. I would prefer to die in the ring, and die proudly, than give up.' Johnny shook his head, 'No, Kostya. I'm in the corner to protect you. If I ever think you're in danger, I will throw in the towel. I don't care if that means you will leave me. I'll still do my job.' I now understand and respect Johnny for such honesty. He would have preferred to end our relationship in order to make sure I was not in danger.

Once the fog of pain started to clear someone asked me why I was now an ex-champion. Because I lost. It was as simple as that. I just didn't fight well. I don't recall saying it — but apparently I suggested that some day I would like to have a rematch for the title and would provide a much better showing. I am also told that I managed a smile, which is the last thing I felt like doing. Vlad took me to hospital to get my cuts sewn up and to make sure there was no unseen damage. The media were waiting at the Atlantic City Medical City. 'What can I say, it just wasn't Kostya's night,' Vlad told them. 'The better fighter won.' While he was talking to the press, Phillips arrived at the same hospital. He, too, needed plenty of work on his battered and bruised face. However, he had the balm of knowing he was now world champion.

Looking back — and isn't hindsight wonderful — I realised there were problems with my diet. I used to have just one meal a day, dinner. For breakfast I would have a cup of black coffee. For lunch I would have a glass of water. I hardly drank any liquids at all. Okay, so it kept my weight down, but it was a terrible mistake, for which I would pay dearly. I had been taking amino acids that were sup-posed to boost my performance, but the lack of water meant excess amino acids were not flushed from my body.

I soon found out why I had been so weak in the fight. Ten days after the fight I was still badly dehydrated, despite drinking copious amounts of water. I asked my doctor: 'What's wrong with me?' He took blood tests and came to the conclusion my diet and lack of water had left me with a high level of amino acids in my body. If I were to box again I would have to look closely at my food and liquid intake. Physical problems like that could be easily addressed. The mental problems would provide a far greater test!

VINCE 'COOL' PHILLIPS (USA)	
World title fight	
WBA welterweight	
12 April 1996	L TKO3 Ike Quartey at Marigot, St Maarten
Other title fight	
IBF intercontinental light-welterweight	
9 April 1992	W Pts12 Harold Brazier at Las Vegas, USA

I had a bad feeling about the fight well before Kostya stepped into the ring. I didn't think his preparation was right, and I told him so, but Kostya was, as always, supremely confident. Sadly, my gut feeling proved to be spot-on! It was a ferocious fight and Kostya was well and truly beaten. It was awful to see him after the fight, he was really sick. When he went to hospital he was very distraught (but then again so, too, was Phillips who was also at the hospital). Kostya was hit with about five or six punches more than he should have taken. I should have thrown in the towel before the referee stopped the fight, but I had difficulty seeing the whole ring from the corner. I was jammed in, and the spot where Phillips had him trapped was out of my vision. Had I seen what was happening, I most certainly would have called it off. That's part of my job — to make sure my fighters don't suffer unnecessary punishment.
— *Johnny Lewis*

The Phillips fight changed everything for me. The omens were bad. When I flew to Atlantic City to be with Kostya I was two months pregnant with Nikita, and I was little help to him at a time when he needed so much mental support. I had trouble sleeping and I was suffering from terrible morning sickness.

Then came that awful result in the fight. It was the worst night of my life. It went 10 rounds and he was getting a beating. It had never happened before and I did not know how to take it. The crowd around me roared at the sight of every drop of blood. I wondered what made civilised people get so excited about watching a man get overpowered by a torrent of punches. At one stage I wanted to jump into the ring and stop the fight — but I knew I never could. I was sobbing by the end of the fight, but I quickly dried my tears before I went into the ring. 'Don't cry, Natasha,' I told myself. 'Don't cry.' I knew Kostya needed me to be strong. He'd always told me that: 'Be strong, Natasha. Always be strong.' So I held in my emotions as I cuddled my beaten hero.

I have never again watched any of his fights — either at the stadium or on television. On the morning of a fight I go to the local Russian Orthodox Church and pray that my Kostya will be a winner and that he will not be hurt. I suppose it is a lot like wives during wartime. They go to church and pray that their husbands, fighting at the front, will live and return to continue their everyday lives.

When the fight starts, I leave the hotel or the house and go for a walk, quietly praying that everything will be okay. Timophey will watch on television with the family. If I come back too early, he will call out, 'Don't come in, Mama, the fight is still on, but don't worry, Papa is all right. He's doing well.' And I will quickly leave and resume my walking. I know it will always be that way until Kostya retires. He needs me around for support, but sadly I will never forget the Phillips fight. It is etched in my mind forever.

Kostya was shattered mentally by the defeat — more than he possibly would admit to himself at the time. What followed was the hardest period of our marriage. He retreated into a shell. Not once did he talk about the fight. It was his personal torture. We all knew not to mention it. When Kostya was ready to talk he would.

He would stay by himself for most of the day. Sometimes he would sit in a chair for hours just staring ahead — staring at nothing and saying nothing. Kostya wanted desperately to cry. You could see it in his eyes. They were full of tears, but his pride would not let him shed even one single tear. Not one! We didn't know what to do. We would take him on picnics but, whereas in the past he would be like an excited kid, now he just wandered away and sat quietly looking at the sky, lost in his own little world, but there was always someone around just in case he suddenly decided to start talking. We hoped that eventually he would.

Kostya also refused to exercise. This was so unlike him. All his life he had kept fit. Even when he was not in full training for a fight he would still work out in the gym or go for a run. Now he just sat around the house and got big and fat. If and when he came around and wanted to fight again it was going to take a superhuman effort to shed all that excess fat.

I don't know what the catalyst was, but eventually he began to spark. The tears were no longer in the eyes. He started talking again, and he began some basic exercises. The cheeky Kostya of old slowly returned, and we all knew that, one day, he would be back in the ring again fighting for (and winning) a world title.

— *Natasha*

VINCIT QUI SE VINCIT

I read a Latin phrase recently. *Vincit qui se vincit.* The translation is: 'He conquers who conquers himself'. It could very well be my motto, because in the wake of my defeat in Atlantic City it was up to me to conquer myself. To put to rest all my fears, to prove that the Phillips debacle was a mere aberration.

In retrospect I realise that I was broken mentally before the fight. It is something that had never happened to me before and has never happened since. I had spent far too much time worrying about the court case. And when you don't concentrate 100 per cent on your preparation you are mentally unprepared. There is that little microchip in your brain that tells you to think only about the fight to the exclusion of everything else, but coming into the Phillips fight that microchip was telling me to think about the court case, at the expense of the fight. When it was over and I had been beaten, that microchip continued to play tricks on me. My first reaction was to retire immediately. That would be the simplest thing to do. The easy way out. But that was also the coward's way. I couldn't give up so easily. For one, it would have played into Bill Mordey's hands. He had said he was going to send me back to Russia with nothing. Not even a rouble. If I retired that was probably what would happen. I would slink off into the night, a sad caricature of a fallen hero.

There was another reason. All the people who had given me their support. Natasha. My family. Johnny Lewis and the team. Vlad. I couldn't walk out on them. I couldn't bear to see the disappointment in their eyes, and see it for the rest of my life.

They all said they would leave the decision up to me and would stand by me in whatever I decided. Johnny just squeezed my arm and said, 'Call me when you're ready.'

I had gone home with a copy of the video of the fight in my suitcase. When I unpacked at Sans Souci I put the video in the bookshelf near the television set. It is still there today and it will stay on the bookshelf forever like some memorial plaque. I have never watched the video. I had no need to watch it, and I will never have such a need. The answer to the question as to why I lost was nowhere on that video. It was in my mind.

The fight was in May 1997. In September I knew I was ready. I called Johnny on the phone as he had suggested. I told him I was ready to continue my quest to become the greatest boxer of my generation.

Vincit qui se vincit. He conquers who conquers himself.

When we first arrived back I was adamant Kostya should give the game away. I was worried about the awful beating he had taken. He had had a full-on boxing career since he was 10 years of age and he was coming up for his 29th birthday. That was an awful lot of boxing. He had recovered well from the initial battering but what was going through my mind was his future health

and welfare. If he hung up his gloves at that time he would still be able to look back on his career and say with pride, 'I was the world champion both as an amateur and a professional'. Not many boxers can say that! We had a meeting, I don't remember exactly when it was, it was a fair time after our return. Vlad, Kostya, Boris, me and a few others. I said my piece. I told them I had to accept some of the blame for the defeat as I had made a few mistakes. Then Kostya spoke. 'I want to fight again,' he said. 'And I want you all to know I take full responsibility for the loss. No one else was to blame.' Kostya put his hand up and accepted the complete liability for the defeat. It was a very brave thing to do. It would have been very easy for him to have offered excuses — but he didn't. In general, Kostya finds it difficult in his nature to come out, shake a person's hand or slap him on the back and say thank you. This was his way of saying thank you to those involved. And we knew we couldn't desert him.
— *Johnny Lewis*

Kostya proved what a real champion he was after the defeat by Vince Phillips. When you are world champion, no matter who you are, you think you are invincible. So it is very hard to handle the unexpected defeat. Invariably, the beaten champions make excuses. They blame everyone except themselves. That's a fairly natural reaction, but Kostya was different. He accepted defeat graciously and then went away and looked at himself in the mirror. That's so very hard, but Kostya did it. He looked for answers not excuses. And when he found those answers he went away and got on with the job of rebuilding his career. That he did so — and did so with such success — is a measure of Kostya's greatness.
— *Jeff Fenech*

It was going to be a case of 'Back to the Future' if I was going to once again wear a world championship belt. Flicking through my diaries I realised I was no longer planning each and every fight. There was none of the complete written preparation that featured in the diaries I kept through my amateur days. I wouldn't commit to paper my ideas of how I thought I would handle my opponents. There was none of the self-assessment after each fight, where I would mark myself out of five. In fact, after most of the fights I never even bothered to write down anything about the bout. And my whole training regimen had changed. I was reminded of one of the many quotes of Dale Carnegie. The successful man will profit from his mistakes and try again in a different way. I was now going to go about regaining my world title, in a different way.

First off all, I needed to prepare in a training camp. In my amateur days I would move from training camp to training camp. From Serov into the Ural Mountains. From Moscow to the Black Sea. Each one different, but each one providing an atmosphere in which there was total concentration on the task ahead. I had heard about the Australian Institute of Sport (AIS) campus, near Black Mountain in Canberra. I needed just one short visit to realise this was what I needed to get back on track. There was a 'camp' atmosphere like I was used to in Russia. What was a real bonus was the fact that there were about four or five world champions in other sports training at the AIS. They included the great Russian swimmer Alexander Popov and Australia's Michael Klim.

Popov had followed his coach, the controversial Gennadi Touretski, from Moscow after Touretski had been signed up by the AIS. Popov had won gold medals in the 50-metre and 100-metre freestyle events at the 1996 Atlanta Olympics. We were to become good friends. Just having him, Klim and the others around provided great support for me in my fight back to the top. Until I stayed at the AIS for the first time, I had lost all motivation. I didn't want to get up in the morning for training. I didn't want to put my body through the agony needed for ultimate success, but once I saw the kids in action at the AIS the motivation returned. Not that I needed help from outside. I was the only one who could black out the pain of defeat and start again from scratch ... not my parents, not Natasha, not Johnny Lewis, not these elite athletes and these world champions. Also at the AIS was Michael Khmel, the former Russian national athletics sprint coach. He helped put me through many sessions of sprinting, aimed at toning up my reflexes.

There was also a problem of an injury to my right eye suffered in the Phillips fight. A muscle in the eye wasn't working properly. I couldn't make any rapid eye movements, an essential for any top-class boxer. I consulted an ophthalmologist who explained that it needed time for the muscles to repair themselves. It could take a couple of months, a year, maybe up to three years. 'It depends how desperately you want to have it working normally,' he added. I was desperate. I had no intention of waiting a couple of years before I could fight again. After undertaking exercises two or three times a day I had it back to normal within a month. These exercises basically involved focusing on something up close and then quickly switching to focus on something in the distance. A simple procedure, but one that had to be repeated over and over again.

My body decided for me when it was time to start back in training. It shouted to me, 'You need exercise.' That was the best thing about the AIS. You had no need to think about transport. You had no need to think about food. You were on the spot and all your meals were laid on. All you had to think about was training.

My day went something like this. Wake up just before dawn. Go for a run as the sun was rising. After about an hour stop for breakfast. Have a short sleep of about 40 minutes to an hour. Take part in a training session for a couple of hours. Have lunch. Have another short sleep. Back to training for another couple of hours. Have dinner. Relax by sitting down with Papa, who acted as my unofficial trainer, and preparing the timetable for the next day.

Everything was there including a gym the size of a soccer field. One day I would work on my triceps and biceps. The next it was the turn of the shoulders and back. Maybe a workout on the running machine the following day. It was just pure concentrated hard work. After two weeks I was buggered. Five or six hours every day in hard training. That's why I needed to sleep three times a day. Within five minutes of my head hitting the pillow I would be in deep sleep. Strangers would ask, 'What are you taking to enable you to train so hard?' There was no need to take anything. There was the goal I had set myself — to win back my world crown.

Papa was there to help me keep my mind on the job. If I slept too long he would wake me and force me back to my training. He was still as tough a taskmaster as he ever was. He knew the limits of my physical endurance. When I would cry out, 'I've had enough!' he would ignore my pleas and drive me harder. He had seen me beaten and was as determined as I was to never let it happen again. 'Rubbish,' he would cry. 'Push yourself harder, Kostya. Push yourself more than any of your opponents would ever think of pushing themselves. It hurts, but it doesn't hurt as much as defeat.'

I would always train to music, some good pop music such as Pink Floyd or some old Russian classics. Anything to inspire non-stop running and punching. Music with drum beats was always good. I could pace myself to the pulsating beat.

I was different to most of the elite athletes at the AIS. Most of them were at the institute on a full-time basis, taking advantage of the dozens of world-renowned coaches under the AIS auspices. I went there for a couple of weeks' concentrated effort using the superb facilities available.

There have been stories of how I took the best training techniques of the other AIS champions and adapted them for my own use. This is pure garbage. Almost everything the others were doing at the AIS I had done at some stage back in Russia. You have to remember that the Soviet Union spent a lot of money ensuring its athletes had only the latest training techniques. I had developed my own system of training and it was working for me now that I was back in the old 'training camp' atmosphere. I also had a dietician prepare a new plan for my meals — three times a day. Not the old dinner-only diet.

I left Canberra knowing I was ready for the first day of the rest of my life. My training regimen and revised diet plan were in place ready to enhance the next stage in my career.

There is a proverb that people should take to heart. Eat to live, not live to eat. Although it rings especially true in the case of sportspeople, it is equally as important for the average person in the street. Sadly, too few people follow the advice.

I suppose by any normal standards, I eat pretty boring meals. I have no choice, especially when I am in my full training regimen, but after all these years, I have got used to it. The major difference between my normal day-to-day eating habits when I'm not in full training is that I allow myself a bit of fat. I'll drink normal milk instead of fat-free milk. The same with yoghurt. I may have a bit of sour cream as dressing for my salads instead of just vinegar.

I eat a lot of meat, with the fat removed, and barbecued. Plenty of pasta and potatoes (the latter either steamed or dry baked in the oven). I stop the meat about five days before a fight. I also cut out most fish. This is because when you eat fish you tend to drink a lot of water. Water adds a lot to your weight and I have to trim my weight before each bout. Indeed, my weight jumps around 15 kilograms when I am not in full training. That's almost a quarter of my fighting weight. It sounds a lot, but it really isn't. A lot of it is because of the two to three litres of water I drink every day. I also love a few beers. Wine, too, but they have too much sugar which puts on weight. A month before a fight, my beer consumption becomes almost taboo. Perhaps just a glass of beer with dinner and then for the final two weeks nothing.

I miss chocolates. And I miss a Russian delicacy that consists of small cubes of pork fat, treated with salt, pepper and herbs. When I'm not fighting I indulge myself, buying the pieces from the local

Russian deli and adding a few extra herbs of my own liking. Yummy!

Of course, I make sure there is never a fight in the pipeline when my birthday comes around every September or when Natasha celebrates her birthday in July. In good old Russian tradition, when we have a birthday we have a big party.

When fight time approaches, the whole family supports me. Natasha and the kids all eat the same food as me. They know it would be such a temptation if I saw them eating something different. Papa does, too. When I train for a fight he loses around five or six kilos. Of course, he doesn't have to ration the size of his portions of food or the amount of water he can drink, but he sticks with my boring diet. It's not a question of him accepting it. He says, 'That's why I am here, Kostya. I'm here for you. I'm here to support you in everything you do.'

People ask me about vitamin supplements. If you are eating a proper diet you should not need vitamins, but because of my intense training schedule I lose a lot of vitamins through my constant sweating. So I stay on a course of multivitamins and sometimes some extra Vitamin B or some Vitamin C.

When I am not in full training I still keep up with my exercises. I do some weights, an hour or so on the walking machine, some stomach exercises and a bit of tennis. When I eventually finish my fighting career I still aim to continue a solid training schedule. With this in mind our new house has a pool, tennis court, gymnasium, sauna and spa. Nearby is a park in which I can ride a bike or go for a run. And I have a squash court at my gym in Rockdale.

The world title loss also accelerated putting into action the plans I had to open my own boxing establishment nearer to home. The Newtown gym served its purpose, but I was spending an hour and a half travelling to and from the gym. I wanted something closer to home, and something that I could turn into a business after I retired as a boxer, and so The Tszyu Boxing Academy was born.

I found the ideal place in the St George Police Citizens Youth Club at nearby Rockdale, a short trip from my home at Sans Souci. There was a little-used gymnastics room that was ideal for the gym. The deal suited both the club and me. The academy opened in early 1998. I brought Chernya out from Serov to be head trainer. My brother-in-law Igor was also given a work permit by the Australian government to come out, with Olga, to be his offsider. I hoped Chernya would teach Igor the tricks of the trade.

After just four months Chernya threw in the job. He said he was homesick and wanted to go home. I was terribly disappointed. I had given him the opportunity to start a new life and make a name for himself in Australia — just as many Russian coaches had at the AIS in Canberra. He had taught me to be tough and to never give up. Yet here he was, giving up at the first hurdle.

Perhaps Chernya was scared starting a business from scratch. It was going to take a lot of time before youngsters were lining up to join the team. In Russia he did not have to worry about such things. Working for the government is much easier. If kids did not come along to learn boxing, he still had a job. Maybe he was embarrassed that his former pupil was now his boss. Suddenly Igor found himself in charge, and he made a good fist of it. It is just sad that he did not get the chance to learn from Chernya. It will be Igor that gets the kudos instead when the young kids work their way through the academy. We already have a few showing some promise, but it will be four or five years before they will be at a stage where they can try out for Olympic selection.

At the same time I was setting up the academy, I realised I had to set up a whole team to manage my future outside the boxing ring. Vlad had acted as my manager since the split with Bill. But Vlad's burgeoning career as a promoter kept him in the United States for long periods and he had less and less time to spend with me. Of course, I had Johnny Lewis looking after my training, but I had tried to fight basically as an individual. I took too much responsibility on my own shoulders. It was like the natural development of a human being. A baby starts to crawl, then walk, then run. I had been walking, but I needed to run. The loss had made me a much wiser man and I realised that if I was to 'run' fast, I needed a good team around me. To be financially successful I needed a top support group. Team Tszyu was born.

Papa didn't agree. He would say to me, 'Kostya, I don't care what you get outside the ring. The important thing is to train hard and be the best in the world.' He has come around to my way of thinking as I look to the future. There is now a small but busy team, from business manager Susie Bennell to media and marketing people. Creating this team was an added responsibility, for when I was fighting, I wasn't just fighting for myself and my family but for Team Tszyu as well.

RETURN TO THE RING

Ismael Chaves was going to think he'd been
run over by the Cannonball Express.
— Johnny Lewis

There was an extra incentive to do well in my 'comeback' fight. I was matched with the Argentine champion Ismael Chaves, who was rated No. 3 contender for the WBC world title. The famed Mexican Julio Cesar Chavez would fight his countryman Miguel Angel Gonzalez for the crown vacated by Oscar de la Hoya who had moved up a weight division. The WBC had decided our bout at Stocklands Stadium in Townsville (the home of the North Queensland Cowboys Rugby League side) would be an eliminator for the right to fight the winner.

Chaves had a fine record of 36 wins and three draws from his 43 appearances in the ring. He hadn't been beaten in the previous five years, although most of the bouts had been against local opponents in his native land. According to reports we had received from America, no fighter had ever been able to knock him off his feet. Needless to say, I hoped to be the first to achieve that distinction. He had no real marks on his face, which indicated a good defensive ability. Another challenge for me was to penetrate those defences. I expected him to be tough, but I would be tougher because I had a point to prove not just to the boxing world, but to myself. I had made a mistake and lost my title, and nothing was going to stop me from winning it back.

The Argentine was quite secretive about all he did after arriving in north Queensland. His sparring partners were his brothers Ariel and Carlos. Ariel was the Argentine welterweight champion and had only lost a couple of fights in an impressive career. Carlos, a lightweight, was not as experienced, but they provided strong opposition for Chaves' preparation. Often they would train away from the prying eyes of photographers and boxing 'groupies' on the roof of their Townsville hotel. On other occasions they were driven away to a secret training camp on the outskirts of the city. This didn't worry me in the slightest. I was super confident. I had never felt so self-assured and convinced I would win since my amateur days. Johnny and I had seen a tape of Chaves and realised he was fast and elusive, but that's what I wanted. A real test to prove I had cleared my mind of the Phillips debacle. Chaves was a southpaw, so we had brought across two good left-handers from the United States to spar with me. They would both also fight on the undercard.

First there was 'Sugar Ray' Collins, a handy 32-year-old, who, a couple of years earlier, had dropped a points decision to Jan Piet Bergman, one of my victims the previous year. The other was the man I had beaten for the IBF world title, Jake 'The Snake' Rodriguez. I had promised him I would use him in the future as a thank you for his sportsmanship after losing the world crown.

Johnny Lewis explained to the media gathered in Townsville,

'Good sparring is the icing on the cake. Ismael Chaves is a southpaw. It is like when you are going to play [Australian tennis legend] Rod Laver, you want to be practising with a left-hander. That's why we invited Jake and Ray. Boxers are always wanting to be around just in case the opportunity presents itself again. They're more than sparring partners, you've got to say that about them. They are so tough and full of hope.'

Sadly that hope was not to be fulfilled. The two Americans would fight Filipinos who had been involved in the Aussie fight circuit during 1997. Collins was to beat a bloke called Dindo Canoy, but it hardly helped enhance his career. Rodriguez unfortunately was to suffer defeat at the hands of a fellow named Ramil Mercado, virtually spelling the end of his career.

Rodriguez told reporters of his confidence in my ability to exorcise the memories of the Phillips fight: 'I don't think Kostya's going to have another bad day. He's doing a good job of staying on our outside. He comes in with his right, then comes in with a hook. He's thinking a lot. He's training so hard. In the two-and-a-half years since I fought him, the improvement has been astronomical. His defence is so much better. There is so much extra power in his punches. He moves so well and so few punches land on him. There will be no more bad days for Kostya Tszyu.'

The bookmakers felt the same way. They had me down as a red-hot favourite at 6-1 on. Vlad urged caution. 'Don't forget Vince Phillips was a 20-1 outsider when he fought Kostya,' Vlad told a media conference. 'But having said that, he has so much more energy this time. I think he is a much better man for the loss. Indeed, we are all much wiser.'

Johnny Lewis was very demanding of me. He didn't just want me to win. He wanted me to win impressively.

 I didn't want to put too much pressure on Kostya, but I made it clear he had to win brilliantly. He had to do so to recapture the

imagination of the boxing public. I wasn't asking him to knock out Chaves — after all, the Argentine kid was a tough nut, but I told the press that if Kostya managed to hit him with a couple of clean shots, Ismael Chaves was going to think he'd been run over by the Cannonball Express. I really had a buzz about Kostya. He had a long, hard preparation, and I pushed him beyond the limits of any ordinary man. He would be very tired and we'd force him to train on regardless. He had every right to hate me for the way I pushed him, but Kostya never once whinged. That was a good sign. No whingeing. Not even a hint of a whinge. You could see he wanted success so much.
— *Johnny Lewis*

I had no trouble in convincing Johnny I was back. Even before I jumped in the ring, I knew I was boss. There was no way I was going to lose. When the bell sounded for Round One, I went out to cut Chaves down to size. I didn't just beat him, I destroyed him. How he survived the first two rounds I will never know, but in the third it was the finish. Bang, bang, bang. Down he went and it was all over. A world title fight was now mine for the taking. Unfortunately it was put on the backburner when in March the following year Chavez and Gonzalez fought a controversial draw in Mexico City. The title was still vacant. In the meantime I had to keep in peak fitness with fights against the top contenders. One by one I would pick them off until my time came.

Meanwhile another likely prospect joined Team Tszyu. Natasha gave birth to Nikita on 19 January 1998. Another beautiful, wonderful son. We had been doubly blessed.

The Chaves fight was supposed to be a world title eliminator, but American fight politics was such that I now had to have yet another 'eliminator' and pay the three per cent of the purse for the 'privilege'.

We needed an opponent with a big name. Not too big, but big enough, and we found him in American Calvin Grove.

Earlier in his career Grove, himself a former world feather-weight champion, had pushed the great Azumah Nelson to a close points decision in a world super-featherweight title bout. He had also effectively ended the careers of two former Australian world champions, Jeff Fenech and Lester Ellis. Grove had knocked out Jeff in the seventh round of their Melbourne bout in June 1993, and three months later he had beaten Lester on points in the same city. Grove and Ellis met again in Melbourne in April 1996, with Grove winning when the referee stopped the bout in the fourth round. The American had fought only one bout in the two years since then, inflicting only the second defeat of his career on a useful fighter named Arturo Gatti, in Atlantic City. Grove could very well be rusty and getting on at 35 years of age, but he was most certainly a dangerous opponent.

I had promised the people of Newcastle I would return — and this was my chance.

CALVIN GROVE (USA)

World title fights
IBF featherweight

23 January 1988	W KO4	Antonio Rivera at Gamaches, France
17 May 1988	W Pts15	Myron Taylor at Atlantic City, USA
4 August 1988	L Pts15	Jorge Paez at Mexicali, Mexico
30 March 1989	L TKO11	Jorge Paez at Mexicali, Mexico

WBC super-featherweight

7 November 1992	L Pts12	Azumah Nelson at Stateline, USA

WBC lightweight

13 December 1994	L KO6	Miguel Angel Gonzalez at Albuquerque, USA

Fights against Australians

7 June 1993	W TKO7	Jeff Fenech at Melbourne, Australia
6 September 1993	W Pts10	Lester Ellis at Melbourne, Australia
30 April 1996	W TKO4	Lester Ellis at Melbourne, Australia

$4 MILLION KNOCKOUT BLOW

Friends tell me that had I read that famous Aussie children's book, I may have not been so trusting of the Australian legal system. All I can say is my experience with the courts taught me a lot about the nuances of the English language and even more about the trust I bestowed on others. To put it bluntly I lost faith in the legal system because of the Mordey court case.

It was just nine days before the fight against Grove when Justice Bainton handed down his verdict. I was in Newcastle training for the fight and Vlad had tried to keep the news from me. But it was to no avail. When I heard what the judge had decided and what he said about me, I just couldn't believe it. Justice Bainton found that I had breached my contract with Bill Mordey and I was ordered to pay more than $7 million in damages — $7,310,445 to be exact. I was astounded.

Bainton described my time in the witness box as 'an exhibition of extraordinary petulance'. He went on to say, 'Tszyu had, in my opinion, become what is connoted by that well-known Australian expression "a spoiled brat". He treats that which favours him as true and that which he does not as false. There are numerous examples of this in his evidence.' Bainton did, however, throw out the case against Vlad, Jeff and the others.

I was amazed that the judge called me 'a spoiled brat'. I have always been taught to respect my elders, to respect age, but how can I be expected to respect a man who makes such a judgement after just hearing me give evidence in the witness box for a few hours? How could he tell what I am like as a person? Even Bill said he was upset at the judge's comments. Surely that says a lot about it.

I am certain the court never really understood the business of boxing. How could the judge have ever arrived at the figure he did? I still shake my head in disbelief. For Bill to have made $7 million out of me in two years I would have had to have earned $35 million. Such a figure was no more than a fantasy. I turn to that famous Aussie expression when asked what chance I had of making $35 million in two years after my first world title win. Buckley's and none! Of course, as the best in the world I should get big money, but that big? There were three junior-welterweight champions, and about 50 world champs when you take into account each weight division, but there is only so much cake to go around all these fighters. Thirty-five million dollars for Kostya Tszyu? I think not.

I learned a lot about the English language when I was in the witness box. I felt that Bill's barrister was a real browbeater. My parents have always taught me to be polite, but I was pushed to breaking point by the cross-examination in the witness box. I asked Bill's barrister not to shout at me. I was ready to politely answer any polite questions, but no one should have to put up with a lawyer raising his voice at him or her. As I said, I learned a lot during the court case and I choose my words very carefully these days. If I am not sure of the nuance in English I will often try to find the exact translation, although, as with any language, some words mean many things when translated.

Looking back at my traumatic time in court I have this memory of the proceedings being a theatre for barristers — a theatre in which they can act out their legal niceties. After meeting with my barrister before the proceedings began I was convinced by the evidence he would offer on my behalf that I had a cast-iron case. I know Bill, too, came away from meetings with his barrister convinced he would win. It was then up to a third lawyer, in this case the judge, to decide who was right. Coming from Russia where such legal arguments would never be countenanced, I found it quite bewildering ... and still do. I keep asking myself 'Where is justice?'

Of course, we appealed against the decision. So did Bill, he was unhappy the others weren't found responsible. As Bill said after Justice Bainton's decision: 'It's going to be a chess game. Commonsense tells you it's going to be hard getting the money off one bloke.' The appeals were heard over five days in April and May 1999 and the judgement was handed down on 13 September. The presiding judges threw out my appeal but also implicated Sky Channel this time. It meant the television network and I would have to share the damages bill, which was rising at around $2000 per day. In December Sky paid the whole amount and then looked to me for my share.

Bill expressed confidence about his future claiming he would win two world titles within a year with his fighters, Shannan Taylor and Lovemore Ndou. Sadly for Bill, neither lived up to his expectations.

People often ask me how I feel about Bill. After all, his court action has cost me $4 million (my share of the damages plus interest), a figure that most people can only dream about. 'You must surely hate Mordey,' people will suggest. I can honestly say I don't. I forgive Bill. His emotions took over at the time we split. It wasn't Bill speaking, it was his emotions. That's why he said things that he probably now regrets. How many times in life do we say, 'I wish I hadn't said that'? Sometimes it's good to swallow your tongue before you start talking. The words are like birds. You open the cage door and they're gone, and you can't get them back.

Hindsight is also a wonderful thing. If only we could see so clearly with foresight. The break with Bill Mordey was inevitable now. I know that. I also know I went about the split in the wrong way. I feel guilty that I upset Bill. I feel guilty that I upset the relationship between Bill and Johnny Lewis (they have never spoken again to this day). I feel guilty that I hurt the relationship between Brian Mills and Johnny. That's what I feel guilty about, but I don't feel guilty about making the break.

The major result of the court judgement is that I find it hard today to trust anyone. When I came to Australia I trusted everyone. I was brought up in a family whose word was their bond. I relied on people telling me the truth. If you do this, Kostya, you will get this. If you don't do this, you will pay this. Everything has changed. These days when people tell me something, my first reaction is that I don't believe it. People now have to earn my trust, and that can often take a long time. I've put up a shutter and closed my life off to people. When I do this I don't like myself, but I don't feel guilty because it's the only way I can see to protect myself.

The only people inside that barrier are my wife and family, my parents and a few close friends. I know they will never dud me, never. I know that their love and friendship will survive any circumstance, any arguments. They accept me for who I am and I accept them unconditionally. I make mistakes. I'm not perfect. Natasha is not perfect, but I love her for what she is. Arguments don't make any difference. Our love does not come with conditions.

I had let worry about the court case torpedo my mental preparation for the Phillips fight, and I had paid the ultimate price. It had cost me my title. I was determined there would not be a repeat this time around. What is the Spanish expression? *Que Sera Sera*. Whatever will be, will be. I had to block the case out of my mind. After all, I couldn't change anything that had happened. The anger I felt about the judge's comments worked to spur me on as I was about to face up to Grove on 5 April 1998. I was determined to prove I was back with a vengeance.

Grove did not know what had hit him. The fight had been underway for just five seconds when I caught him with a solid right, the first I had thrown. He went down in a heap. It caught me by surprise. I didn't expect it to happen so quickly. He got up and tried to dance away. I followed him around the ring and hurt him with some solid punches. He was very courageous and refused to go down. After a minute or so I put him down again. This time when he got up I chased him until he was pinned against the ropes. Bang, bang, bang. Lefts and rights caught him and shook him. A right to the side of the head finished it all off and the referee stopped the bout with about a second left in the first round. Grove's team helped him back to the corner but it was some time before he was able to stand up unaided.

I spoke from the ring to the 6500 fans telling them not to think Grove was a second-rate fighter and reminded them of what he had done to Jeff and Lester. To beat him I had to be at the top of my form. I told them that even though I had been to Newcastle many times, this victory was very special, and I hoped to return with another world title and defend my crown in front of them.

Grove was kind in his words after the fight, 'Every time he punched me my legs went from under me. He was too strong and too big for me. To lose to Kostya Tszyu is no shame. This will be my last fight. By the way he embarrassed me Kostya has told me it's time to quit.'

Johnny explained to the reporters, 'I don't think Calvin realised Kostya could hit so hard. I doubt whether there is anyone who can hit as hard — even up to the best fighters in the middleweight division. We have some unfinished business. There is a world title belt to reclaim.'

Not just one belt. I wanted all three — the WBC, WBA and IBF titles.

I would have loved to continue staging my fights in Newcastle, but the bottom line was that the city could not generate sufficient gates. So it was back to the United States, this time to El Paso in Texas, where I would fight Mexican Rafael Ruelas in what was officially listed as a world title eliminator on 15 August 1998. Allegedly the winner of a world title eliminator was guaranteed a shot at the crown, but my fight in Townsville against Ismael Armando Chaves had been listed as an official eliminator, and I was still waiting for my promised title shot. To put it bluntly all the designation 'eliminator' meant was that you paid the WBC three per cent of the purse just for giving the fight their blessing and then hoped they would come through with their side of the bargain and give you a shot at the world championship. Now, against Ruelas, the WBC chiefs were getting their cut again. They kept telling me they were doing me a favour. 'We're looking after you, Kostya,' they would say. What sort of favour is it taking three per cent of your purse time after time? And we're talking about significant amounts of money.

In another irony, the fight was put up for auction to the highest bidder, and who should it be than Bill Mordey, with a bid of $US 1.3 million. Mordey told reporters it was purely a business decision. He said that because I owed him so much money he wanted me to keep winning to make sure I had the money to pay him. Vlad was equally blasé about the deal: 'With that sort of money on offer, I don't care who is promoting the fight. After all, we will be the beneficiaries.'

El Paso was an ideal place to stage such a bout. The city of 650,000 people sits on the US border with Mexico. Just across the Rio Grande is the twin city of Ciudad Juarez, with a population of two million. The fight was assured of attracting a capacity crowd, many of them fervent supporters of Ruelas from over the border.

Ruelas was a good fighter. He was a former IBF world lightweight champion, and it had taken a boxer of the calibre of Oscar de la Hoya to dethrone him. In the previous two years he had remained unbeaten, winning all but one of his nine fights by knockout. The one fellow who had taken him the distance, before being beaten on points, was Livingstone Bramble, who had given me such a tough time in Newcastle back in 1993.

As far as I was concerned, the Mexican was a good bloke. But I'm afraid I can't say the same thing about his management. They caused one hassle after another.

Despite their efforts to distract me from my preparation, I still liked my time in El Paso and would go back again if a decent purse was offered for a fight in that city, but we took no chances. I even had my own cook just to ensure there was no funny business with my meals.

The fight was never in doubt from the moment I caught him with a ruthless right in Round One. It shook him to the core. For nine rounds I stalked him. He took so much punishment but kept coming back for more. He had the wobbles for nine rounds but kept standing. I hit him with every punch I had in my repertoire. I hit him from every angle. With my right, with my left. Punches from underneath his guard, punches over the top. He was so brave. He just retreated, stood against the ropes and took everything I served up. The referee seemed reluctant to stop the fight. He said later that it was such an important bout that he wanted to give Ruelas every opportunity to win, but it was obvious he couldn't and eventually in the ninth round the referee mercifully called it off.

Ruelas never really recovered physically or mentally. A year later he had a fight in Miami against Hicklet Lau, a Cuban with a fairly average record. Ruelas was awarded a points win over 10 rounds, a decision that shocked all the experts who watched the fight, but Ruelas saw the writing on the wall and hung up his gloves.

RAFAEL RUELAS (USA)		
World title fights		
IBF lightweight		
19 February 1994	W Pts12	Freddie Pendleton at Inglewood, USA
27 May 1994	W KO3	Mike Evgen at Las Vegas, USA
28 January 1995	W TKO8	Billy Schwer at Las Vegas, USA
IBF & WBO lightweight		
6 May 1995	L TKO2	Oscar de la Hoya at Las Vegas, USA

CHAMPION ONCE AGAIN

Indio, California, is a small city of around 45,000 people situated south-east of Los Angeles near Palm Springs. It's in the middle of the desert and has been described as 'the sunniest city in the United States' and 'the date capital of the United States'. It was also the headquarters for General George Patton before he went off to do battle in Europe during World War II.

I was there for a battle of my own. My opponent was to have been the Mexican Miguel Angel Gonzalez for the vacant WBC light-welterweight crown. There was plenty of contention about the title. Gonzalez had failed in a gallant bid against Oscar de la Hoya almost two years earlier, beaten by points in Las Vegas. When de la Hoya moved up to the next weight division, Gonzalez was matched with fellow Mexican Julio Cesar Chavez in Mexico City for the vacant title, with the winner to meet me, and that fight ended in an uproar in front of 50,000 screaming fans. Chavez was the darling of the Mexico City fans and if you fought him in that city there was no way you would get the verdict without knocking him out. So it was with Gonzalez. All the keen fight critics who witnessed the encounter reckoned Gonzalez was the better of the pair (even in the many exchanges of below-the-belt blows). He was said to have won eight or nine of the 12 rounds, but the judges gave their decision as a draw. The fans pelted the ring with rubbish and security men were needed to get the boxers back to their respective dressing rooms.

So the title was still vacant and I was to get my chance against Gonzalez on 28 November 1998. He had a warm-up bout, but was unimpressive in beating Alexis Perez, a Cuban exile who had lost seven of his latest 10 fights, on a TKO in the fifth round at San Antonio, Texas, in early July. Two days before I was due to leave home for the flight to America, Gonzalez dropped out. His management said he was injured. Just what the injury was, I've never been able to ascertain. One day they told me it was his ribs, on another occasion it was one of his hands. American friends told me he had been unimpressive in training and his management was afraid their meal ticket would be beaten. It didn't matter. The fight was off.

Luckily the WBC stepped in and offered the fight to Diobelys Hurtado, another Cuban exile living in the United States. He had fled his native city of Santiago in 1994 after an amateur career in which he had 221 bouts (losing 20 of them). Hurtado would be fighting just 15 days after his previous bout (a 10-round points win over a clever Mexican, Manuel Gomez). The Cuban jumped at the chance because the winner of his bout with me would be declared interim world champion, with the proviso that the first defence must be against Gonzalez.

Even though I had been training to take on a boxer with a completely different style of fighting to Hurtado, I was happy with the decision, too. That world title (interim or not) was a big bait. I was lucky that my two sparring partners had both fought against

Hurtado and could give me some inside information on how to handle the Cuban. I was wary about him. Almost two years earlier he had performed well in a challenge for the WBC welterweight title. That was against the renowned Pernell 'Sweat Pea' Whitaker, a four-times world champion. Hurtado had knocked Whitaker to the canvas on two occasions and had outboxed him for 10 rounds. Then with just over a round and a half left, and the title seemingly within his grasp, he was caught by a brutal barrage of blows and the referee stepped in and stopped the fight. Whitaker had pulled off a late triumph.

Hurtado tried to play mind games with me at the weigh-in. He should have known better. Bluster and bluffing never work against me. He demanded changes in the contract (but was rebuffed). He demanded I have new blood tests for hepatitis B and AIDS (and was again told he was out of order). I was feeling confident.

Round One was full of action. I knocked Hurtado down with a solid blow. I then slipped and fell to the canvas, with the crowd roaring because they thought I had been hit. I was hit moments later by a good right hand. Although it forced me off my feet I was unhurt and winked at Johnny Lewis to let him know I was okay, but the blow did cause some visible damage, with a balloon blowing up under my right eye. It looked a lot worse than it felt. We both went at each other, hammer and tongs. In the fifth round I caught him with a real beauty to the body. He went down like a sack of potatoes. He staggered to his feet and tried to defend, but he was gone. About 10 or 12 seconds later the referee stepped in to save him from serious injury.

After the official announcement of my victory, journalists gathered around to question me. Papa had the world championship belt and was holding it up over my head for the photographers. I made it clear that I did not regard myself as an 'interim' champion. I was *the* champion. The reporters laughed when I joked about the huge swelling under my right eye. I told them it was just a scratch. What would winning a world title be without getting a scratch?

Of course, I would have to fight Gonzalez, but I was looking much further down the track than that. When I won in Sydney in 1991 I had been crowned undisputed world amateur champion. Right now I was just one of three world professional champions in my weight division. My goal was to change all that. I was going to unify the titles.

DIOBELYS HURTADO (Cuba)	
World title fight	
WBC welterweight	
24 January 1997	L TKO11 Pernell Whitaker at Atlantic City, USA

BEWARE OF CROCODILES

The deal that allowed me to fight Hurtado for the world title was that the winner would defend the crown against Miguel Angel Gonzalez. Of course, he had pulled out of the original fight at the 11th hour, but when we were due to meet again for my title, there were many, many administrative problems that saw it delayed two or three times. I kept up solid training not knowing just when the bout would take place. Eventually it was set for 21 August 1999.

The delays meant that I had been out of the ring for nine months. This is a long time for a boxer. You can get all the hard work you want in the gym, sparring with tough campaigners, but you are still liable to be a bit rusty if you don't have regular bouts. Gonzalez was at a similar disadvantage. After his controversial drawn bout in Mexico City with Julio Cesar Chavez in March the previous year, he had just the one fight, the TKO in five rounds of Alexis Perez. Gonzalez had been hoping for a rematch with Chavez, a big payday that never eventuated. So he had been out of the ring for 13 months.

America's so-called experts claimed he would land many more punches on me than I would manage to rain on him. He would be there at the finish and would win handsomely on points. They questioned my stamina. I just shrugged off all the questions about my ability to withstand the Gonzalez onslaught. Just wait and see, was what I suggested.

The bout was set down for Miami in Florida. I never liked to fight on America's east coast. It made for a long journey from Australia, having to change planes at Los Angeles. It would always be more than 24 hours from the time I left home until I checked into my hotel at the other end. Sometimes it was a journey of up to 30 hours. Not good.

We were staying on the outskirts of Miami at a town in the Florida Everglades called Miccosukee. It was named after one of the three Indian tribes that once lived in the area — the Miccosukee, the Seminole and the Creek.

We arrived at our hotel in the middle of the night. By the time I unpacked my bags it was almost time to have my first morning training session. It was hot and humid — very unpleasant conditions in which to run. I would do my 'roadwork' along some walking tracks through the Everglades, next to the hotel. I'll never forget the hundreds of frogs that would jump across the track and into the hotel grounds. Huge frogs with incessant croaking provided music for my daily runs. Every hundred metres or so I would hear a big splash that seemed to be just a metre or two into the Everglades. The hotel staff explained that the splashes I had heard were made by large crocodiles, and there was no need to worry about them. It had been years since a croc had attacked anyone. I decided that if I saw one, I would have to pretend I was in the ring and dart out of harm's way.

The Gonzalez camp tried every little trick to upset me. The press

Hard work at the Tszyu Boxing Academy at Rockdale in preparation for the 2001 unification bout with Zab Judah. *Chris McGrath/Allsport*

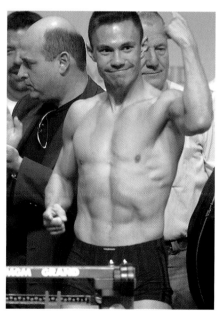

I'm feeling good at the weigh-in for the Zab Judah bout. *AAP Image/John Gurzinski*

Catching Judah unawares. He wanted a confrontation at the weigh-in — but it never came. *AAP Image/John Gurzinski*

Judah realises I'm determined. *AAP Image/Eric Jamison*

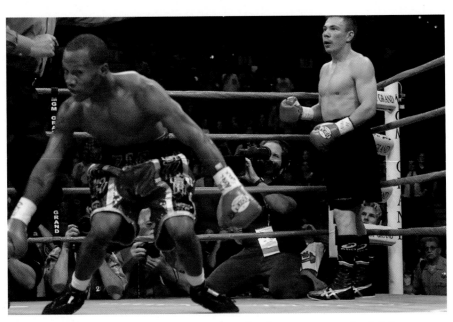

His legs won't respond as he staggers across the ring. *AAP Image/Lori Cain*

Then he's down. *AAP Image/John Gurzinski*

And once the realisation that he's lost sinks in, Judah attacks referee Jay Nady. *Associated Press/Lori Cain*

Winner takes all. I've unified all three world titles. *Associated Press/Lori Cain*

Time for fun — a family break on Hamilton Island

Part of the Tszyu menagerie – my electus parrot, Leha

I cop a head butt from Ghana's Ben Tackie in the first defence of my unified world crown in 2002. *Associated Press/Joe Cavaretta*

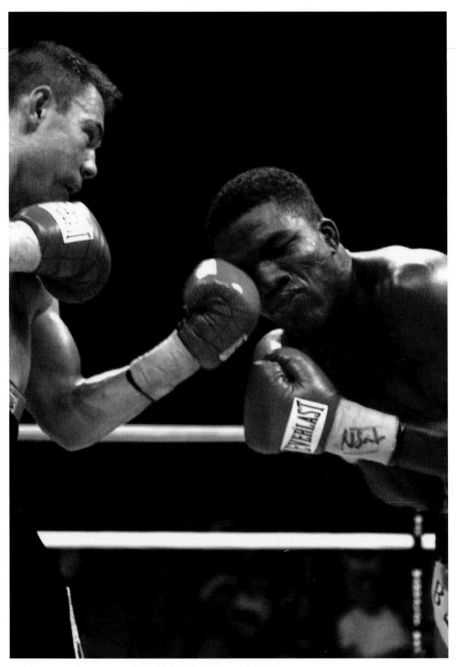

But I give more than a little extra in return. *AFP Photo/John Gurzinski*

After my victory against Sammy Fuentes on Black Friday, 13 November 1992.
Left to right: Papa, Olga, Mama and Natasha

With Aunty Valentina and Timophey at Taronga Zoo. It was my Aunty's first visit to Australia

The grandchildren with Papa and Mama on Papa's 55th birthday

A toast to Mama and Papa on their 35th wedding anniversary in 2001

Olga and Igor join in the celebrations

Smiles all round with members of Team Tszyu after successfully defending my unified world crown. From left: Paul Upham, Susie Bennell, me, and James Ajaka.
Paul Upham

It's good to be home! With Olga, Igor, Daniel (left), Nikita (centre) and Timophey at a celebration dinner with friends and family after the Tackie fight

conference, which was held two days before the fight, degenerated into a farce. I wrote about it in my diary, but I couldn't possibly repeat here the rude words I used to describe it. Let's be polite and just say it was disorganised. First of all, the press conference was delayed by 25 minutes. It was then hijacked by the Gonzalez camp, who played up to the Hispanic media. Eventually I walked out. I told them I wasn't going to miss my scheduled training session for a theatrical farce.

For once I had a bit of trouble getting down to my fighting weight. Whenever I take time off from training my weight can balloon up to about 15 kilograms over the correct weight. Once I get back into full-time training I normally get that off with ease. This time I was having a bit of trouble with the final couple of kilograms, but I knew I would make it. I wanted to check my weight on the official scales, but once again the American promoters wouldn't allow me. I wasn't able to weigh myself until the day of the weigh-in, the promoters told me. The day before the weigh-in I checked on my computerised scales and was 64.9 kilograms before training, 63.3 kilograms after training and 64.2 kilograms after breakfast (one tub of yoghurt, two pieces of bread, a little bit of cereal and 19 grams of water). There would be no problem of getting down to the 63.5 kilograms weight limit by losing my body wastes.

When I went to check on the official scales it seemed I was 700 grams over the limit. It was a big ask to get rid of the excess as I was already dehydrated. Normally after a training session I would drink between two and three litres of water. That morning I had kept it to 100 millilitres. I was forced to take a 45-minute power walk in the hot, humid morning sun, wearing wet-weather gear to help sweat it off. I did so, but I was very angry with the promoters. Had I been able to check the day before and found myself overweight, I would have been able to cut down on my food and liquid intake in the intervening 24 hours and easily make the limit.

At the weigh-in, Gonzalez was confident but not cocky. I liked that. I always wanted my opponents to give me a good fight. It is no challenge to beat an opponent who is not in your class. Gonzalez wasn't as good as I had expected. Brave, yes. Classy, no. From the first minute I knew I would hold onto my title. It was a one-sided fight as I kept hitting him with sharp jabs. My body blows were finding their target and he took more rights to the head than half a dozen of my former opponents put together. He went close to the bone with many suspect blows. I thought a lot of them were low. Often he tried to headbutt me, and I caught several rabbit punches on the back of the neck, but the referee seemed unperturbed. Gonzalez had never been knocked out in any of his 45 previous bouts. Indeed, he had only lost one (to de la Hoya) and had that disputed draw with Chavez. Gonzalez's pride was the only thing that kept him from going down under the avalanche of blows from me.

At one stage in Round Eight, the referee called to Gonzalez's team in the corner to see if they wanted to throw in the towel, but they shook their heads. After another two rounds that's exactly what happened. Gonzalez was still standing, but he was a bloodied and dazed mess. I had hoped he would have gone down much earlier and saved himself all that pain and trauma, but his misplaced pride kept him going and no matter how hard I hit him, he wouldn't concede.

I was told that the well-known boxing agent Dan Majeski later made an official complaint to the World Boxing Council about Gonzalez's trainer Abel Sanchez, for showing no compassion to his fighter. Majeski was reported as saying, 'Gonzalez will never get over that beating. He could have suffered permanent brain damage.' For a while it looked as if Gonzalez would retire after that fight, but the hope of future paydays eventually forced him to change his mind. Sixteen months later he made a return to the ring for a first-round knockout of a patsy, who had lost 12 of his previous

15 fights. He then lost a split decision to former title contender
Manuel Gomez before hammering an unknown Mexican in three
rounds. These days Gonzalez paints a sad picture, nothing like the
champion he was in his prime.

MIGUEL ANGEL GONZALEZ (Mexico)		
World title fights		
WBC lightweight		
24 August 1992	W KO9	Wilfrido Rocha at Mexico City, Mexico
5 December 1992	W Pts12	Darryl Tyson at Mexico City, Mexico
26 April 1993	W Pts12	Hector Lopez at Aguas Calientes, Mexico
13 August 1993	W Pts12	David Sample at Guadalajara, Mexico
27 November 1993	W TKO11	Wilfrido Rocha at Mexico City, Mexico
29 March 1994	W TKO5	Jean Baptiste Mendy at Levallois, France
6 August 1994	W TKO8	Levander Johnson at Juarez, Mexico
13 December 1994	W TKO6	Calvin Grove at Albuquerque, USA
25 April 1995	W Pts12	Ricardo Daniel Silva at South Padre Island, USA
2 June 1995	W Pts12	Marty Jakubowski at Ledyard, USA
8 August 1995	W Pts12	Lamar Murphy at Las Vegas, USA
WBC junior-welterweight		
18 January 1997	L Pts12	Oscar de la Hoya at Las Vegas, USA
7 March 1998	D Pts12	Julio Cesar Chavez at Mexico City, Mexico

Hanging on my lounge room wall in Sydney is a silver and black
sombrero. It was a gift from one of the contenders for my WBC
junior-lightweight title, Ahmed Santos. He gave it to me before our
fight in Uncasville, Connecticut, on 12 February 2000. Perhaps he
thought it was going to be a swap for my world title belt, but there
was no chance of that. It hangs on the wall as a constant reminder

of my torrid battles with Mexicans. Julio Cesar Chavez, Hector Lopez, Miguel Angel Gonzalez and, of course, Santos.

Uncasville is a small town with a population of around 10,000 located around 150 kilometres north-west of New York. Its one and only claim to fame is the Mohegan Sun Casino, where the fight was being staged. We decided against staying in Uncasville, preferring the town of Norwich about 20 minutes away. It was best known as the birthplace of an infamous War of Independence traitor, Benedict Arnold. We arrived in late January, and I immediately wondered why we chose this town and time for the fight. It was the middle of winter and freezing cold.

Santos was the North American junior-welterweight champ and No. 7 contender for the title. While he had only lost two fights in his career and had beaten some good guys he was not in my class and did not pose a real threat. He was just a good boxer who would never give up. We both saw the fight as a stepping stone to bigger pay cheques in the future. I would have to break both my legs before I could lose. It was a chance to enjoy myself in the ring and try out new techniques in the heat of battle. I would practise punches and combinations of punches that I hadn't used in the past. It would have been too dangerous to try such tactics against a great fighter such as Gonzalez, but against Santos it was a different matter. I did make a note in my diary: 'I must remember that every fight is my future. I must not lose. Be smart. Be strong.'

I picked Santos off from afar, trying all my new combinations to great effect and parrying all his attempts at attack. He was as I expected, a tough fellow. I caught him several times on the chin with good solid punches but he did not flinch. In the eighth round I twice knocked him to the canvas. After the second knockdown the referee stepped in and stopped the fight. Santos said after the fight that he had expected me to hit harder. I wondered whether I had eased back because in my subconscious I knew I could easily account for the Mexican.

Zab Judah, the cocky fighter from Brooklyn in New York, fought on the same card, beating Jan Piet Bergman with a fourth-round knockout for the vacant IBF version of the world crown. He jumped into the ring after my bout, ostensibly to congratulate me on successfully defending my title. He had already been bad-mouthing me to local boxing personalities. As he approached I told him he must learn to respect me. 'I do, I do,' he said. But after I had headed off he suggested to the sycophantic local pressmen, 'I respect him, but nothing like the way he's going to respect me when I beat him and unify the titles. He's not a champ. He's a chump!'

AHMED SANTOS (Mexico)		
Title fights		
North American light-welterweight		
16 April 1999	W Pts12	Patrick Thorns at Bossier City, USA
28 August 1999	W TKO5	Cihat Salman at Traverse City, USA

THE ANGEL OF DESTRUCTION

I now had to have my mandatory title defence against the WBC's No. 1 contender, veteran Julio Cesar Chavez. The Mexican would be a formidable opponent. In his native land they called him Angelito, the Angel of Destruction. He had fought 109 bouts over a period of 20 years in the professional ring. He had lost only four times, although two of those losses had been in his most recent five fights. One defeat was in Las Vegas nine months earlier to Willy Wise, who had been beaten in his previous three outings against moderate opponents. Wise won nearly every one of the 10 rounds in their bout to take out a points decision. The other defeat came when he lost his world welterweight crown to the great Oscar de la Hoya in the same city in September 1998. De la Hoya had given him such a pasting that Chavez refused to come out for Round Nine, but he was a tough nut, this Mexican. Only one man had ever knocked him off his feet. That was de la Hoya. I reckoned I could become the second. Willy Wise couldn't knock him down, but Wise was hardly world-class. And Chavez had been fighting as a welterweight for the previous two years and would have to shed a lot of poundage to make the weight for our fight. It would leave him well and truly drained.

A fight of a different kind had to be fought before I even stepped into the ring against Chavez. His promoter was none other than Don King. The Mexican had made millions of dollars for King, and the promoter was looking forward to him making many millions more. Everything in our bout had to suit Chavez. That's the way King works.

King proposed the fight should take place in Mexico City. King had been there before with Chavez, when in February 1993 he had defended his WBC world light-welterweight title against 22-year-old American Greg Haugen. The bout had drawn a crowd of 132,250 to the Azteca Stadium, scene of the 1968 Olympics. It is still the biggest attendance of paying customers for any fight anywhere in the world. Needless to say, Haugen was overwhelmed by the atmosphere with so many Mexicans baying for his blood. Chavez won on a technical knockout in the fifth round.

There was no way we were going to Mexico. Vlad was adamant. 'It's a third world country, anything could happen.' There was also the problem of the high altitude. The Mexico Olympics showed only too well the problems facing sportsmen and women from countries at sea level. People back home told me how the famous Australian distance runner Ron Clarke almost died in Mexico City when he could not cope with the altitude in a race he had dominated with world record after world record at sea level.

Chavez's management had also been known to pull off a few suspect decisions in Mexico. For years all the boxing record books reckoned Chavez had been disqualified in his 12th fight against fellow Mexican Miguel Ruiz, a bout in his hometown of Culiacan. That loss would have spoiled an unblemished record of 90 wins over the first 14 years of his career that he took into a 1994 bout in Las Vegas which he lost to American Frankie Randall. Chavez's publicists claimed the local boxing commission in Culiacan had altered the verdict to a first round knockout victory to Chavez some 24 hours after the fight. It is interesting to note that Ramon Felix, Chavez's manager, just happened to be a member of the Culiacan commission that reversed the result.

Then there was Chavez's only other bout in Mexico City, for the WBC world light-welterweight crown against the man I fought in 1998, Miguel Angel Gonzales. Keen judges said Gonzales won easily, but the match was declared a draw.

Is it any wonder we were wary of the machinations of Don King.

King was playing funny buggers. He refused to take any of Vlad's telephone calls, but Vlad was not easily put off. Someone suggested that all those years Vlad had spent selling cars at Five Dock paid off. He flew to America and tracked King down to a place in Florida. There he buttonholed the flashy promoter.

I was not afraid to confront him. I wasn't scared by his reputation, and I think he respected that, but negotiations were hard. You have to bite your tongue a lot … wait for the right time to jump in. You feel like wading in with a cricket bat, but that will do you no good. He kept demanding Mexico. In turn I said it had to be Australia. Eventually after an hour and a half of mental pushing and shoving he agreed to let me promote the fight wherever I wanted.
— *Vlad Warton*

It was a real coup for Vlad to get the promotional rights. Ever since Chavez had first fought outside Mexico, in 1982, King had promoted all his American bouts. Vlad decided the safest spot for the title defence would be Las Vegas. We usually got a fair go there, but there was an immediate setback. The Nevada State Athletic Commission refused to sanction the fight. They were concerned that I would seriously harm Chavez. They had looked at videotapes of his fight against Wise and decided our bout wouldn't be a fair contest. Even when they were shown Chavez's effort in knocking out American Buck Smith in three rounds in Culiacan after the Wise fight they were unmoved.

What could we do? The WBC had demanded I fight him or lose my title, and even if he was supposedly past his prime he was still a worrying opponent. As I suggested to the 'doubting Thomases', the dying lion is still dangerous. When he is desperate and cornered he could do crazy things. Even a cornered rabbit will scratch and bite. The fact that everyone kept saying Chavez was over the hill just made him angry and doubly determined to prove that he was still a great fighter.

Vlad moved the fight to Phoenix, Arizona, but again he struck trouble. The owners of all the modern, state-of-the-art venues refused to make their arenas available. They were worried about crowd control. Arizona has a huge Mexican population, and, as it was only about 300 kilometres from Mexico itself, a huge influx of excitable fellow countrymen were expected to pour across the border to support their hero. The stadium owners feared a riot if I won the bout. Eventually Vlad arranged for the fight to be on 29 July 2000 at the Veterans Memorial Coliseum, an aging venue that would hold about 18,000.

Despite the way the Nevada officials dismissed Chavez's chances, I was not going to take any risks. I arranged for three top sparring partners, two from Mexico and one from the United States, to come out. In training sessions I would rotate the three of them, ensuring I pushed myself to the very limits of my physical endurance. I also encouraged them to throw low blows at me. I had watched videos of Chavez and knew he threw the low blows with monotonous regularity and usually got away with it. If I wasn't ready and able to fend them off I could be in grave danger.

It turned into a real circus in Phoenix. Chavez was feted by the press as the greatest thing since sliced bread, and he had a right to such a treatment. There is little doubt that he was the finest boxer to ever come out of Mexico. His six different world titles in four weight divisions were testimony to that. Had it not been for de la Hoya, one of the sport's legends, his record would have been even greater. Chavez played to the media. At training he would have half a dozen flunkies pandering to his every need. Every day, the Spanish-language newspapers were full of his predictions of how he planned to dispose of me. A casual observer could have been forgiven for thinking that he only had to turn up at the Coliseum to collect the title belt. The bookmakers in Las Vegas (one of the few places in the United States where you could place a bet legally) thought otherwise. He was quoted as a 50-1 outsider — and there were few takers even at those odds.

Chavez challenged Vlad to bet $US150,000 on me. Vlad just laughed and shook his head. It would be like taking candy from a baby, he told the Mexican, and, anyway, gambling was illegal in Arizona so the pair could end up in jail.

There was also a bit of controversy before the fight. Vlad had signed Willy Wise to fight on the undercard. Chavez reckoned that was planned as an insult to him and threatened to cancel the fight if Wise was involved on the night. Vlad had to agree and poor old Willy missed out on a great evening.

For a while you could have been forgiven for believing our fight was just an afterthought. Another boxer on the undercard was the flamboyant Puerto Rican Hector Camacho Jnr, the No. 1 contender in the WBA listings and unbeaten in his 28 fights (17 of which he had won by knockout). His marketing men had dubbed him 'Macho Man', and he certainly tried to live up to the image. He kept strutting around the lobby of the hotel in which I was staying demanding that I give him a shot at my title. He got plenty of media coverage if only because of the garish sequined suit he wore.

The slightest movement and there was a shimmering wave of sparkles. He was the son of a former world champion, Hector Camacho Snr, who like his son was never short of words.

'I'll even go to Australia to take the title away from Tszyu,' said the brash 21-year-old. 'Kostya is going to whip Julio. The Aussie is too young and too sharp. If he goes in attacking from the start, the fight could be over in no time at all. If Chavez does manage to win, and I can't see how, I'd like a crack at him to avenge the defeat he inflicted on my dad in 1992 in their title fight.'

Camacho Jnr certainly knew how to keep grabbing the headlines. He was accompanied on his journey from the dressing room to the ring by a marching band, and he himself was dragged down the aisle 'riding' a wooden horse. Shades of the siege of Troy, perhaps. He did perform well in the ring, disposing of the former IBF world lightweight champion from South Africa, Philip 'No Deal' Holiday, in six rounds.

I had commissioned a new pre-fight anthem when I had real hassles trying to get permission to use Pink Floyd numbers. New York songwriter Tommy Farragher, who had collaborated on the Rocky theme, had flown to Sydney to work with local writer Nick Howard on the song. To get the right mood they watched me work out at the Rockdale gym, and they came up with a truly inspiring theme song, 'Something Worth Fighting For'. The television-invented Aussie pop band Bardot recorded the song so it could be played in Phoenix.

The beat was a rousing one, and the lyrics summed up the way I felt inside:

Fear me, hear me, dare you come near me,
I'm as hard as rock inside,
And I'm gonna knock you out tonight.

My new theme was played as I entered the ring, but I don't think anyone could hear it. The arena was packed to the rafters with Mexicans, and they booed me from the moment I came into view. Some of the media told me the fans were also yelling 'Matale', Spanish for 'Kill him', but I couldn't hear anything. My mind, as usual, was blocked out. I was concentrating on one thing, the task ahead. I knew I was going to win and nothing the crowd said or did was going to change that.

Don King walked out to the ring with Chavez and the cheers shook the arena. Chavez had his own mariachi band and all the musicians tried to cram into the ring. It was all meant to distract me, but it didn't worry me in the slightest.

Just as I had anticipated, from the start Chavez kept coming in low — often too low. He caught me in the testicles on more than one occasion, but I managed to block the low blows.

As befitting a fighter with such a fine record as he had, Chavez had a great technique and a pretty solid defence. He had obviously prepared well for the fight and seemed in good shape. I was to comment after the fight what a great warrior he was — and I meant it. It took me a while to get him to let down his guard and show me an opening. At first I missed with a few of my rights and also with what should have been solid left hooks.

Slowly, slowly, slowly I worked my way inside his defences. I just kept whipping my left hand into his face. Bang, bang, bang. Chavez had demanded a bigger ring than normal to help him get away from my punches, but no matter how big the ring, there was no place to hide. The low blows became more frequent in the fifth round as Chavez knew his time was nearly over. Early in the next round, the referee deducted a point from his score because of his persistent fouls. Not that it mattered. I was working on his body — punch, punch, punch. Then he dropped his hands. It was all I needed. I hit him with a perfectly timed right to the chin and he went down with a look of amazement on his face. Only once before in his career had that happened. He tried to shake the cobwebs out of his head as he lifted himself off the canvas at the count of seven, but I knew I had him and went in for the kill. Bang, bang, bang. I had him on the ropes with him unable to move his head out of the range of my punches. Ninety seconds into the round, the referee stopped the fight. At exactly the same time Chavez's crew threw in the towel. Their boy had had enough. I reckon I was the first person to knock him down really hard. Yet it wasn't a hard punch. It was just perfectly timed. It snapped into the chin with the speed of a rocket and he had never felt one like it in his long, illustrious career.

I had always wanted to fight this guy. Even back in Russia, I wondered what it would be like getting into the ring with him. After all, he was a world professional champion when I was still in the amateur ranks. One of the greatest names in the history of boxing.

Chavez was gracious in defeat. He praised my effort and suggested his career was over:

> It looks as if it's time for me to retire … I gave my best, but my body did not respond. I am very sad. Forgive me. I apologise to the Latin people. It wasn't a case of me struggling after taking off the weight. No. It's just time for me to leave, to hang up my gloves for good.

Of course, history shows that he had second thoughts about retirement, but it was more than a year before he stepped into the ring again (at Ciudad Juarez in his homeland of Mexico), for a second-round knockout of an aging American, Terry Thomas, whose best fights were in the late 1980s. It is so very sad. Here was Chavez, one of the greatest fighters the world has ever known, and after all those years at the top, and all those multi-million-dollar pay cheques, he was forced to box on because he was stony broke. Promoters and others in the game had ripped him off throughout his career, and no one had taught him how to invest his millions. He had spent like there was no tomorrow and was left with virtually nothing to show for his two decades in the ring.

The Mexicans in the crowd on the night of our fight were not as gracious as Chavez. When the fight was stopped they erupted in anger and threw everything that wasn't screwed down in the direction of the ring. Beer bottles, plastic cups, half-eaten hotdogs rained down on us. There were even some plastic chairs hurled at us. A battalion of security guards under the watchful eye of Glen Jennings from Team Tszyu hustled us to the dressing room. The Mexican fans' reaction didn't matter. I had beaten one of the great names in boxing, and beaten him decisively.

In the aftermath of the fight Camacho Jnr told everyone he wanted to fight me. But I wanted to unify the world titles, and that meant fighting blokes like WBA champion Sharmba Mitchell and IBF champ Zab Judah. Contenders like the 'Macho Man' would have to join the queue.

JULIO CESAR CHAVEZ (Mexico)		
World title fights		
WBC super-featherweight		
13 September 1984	W KO8	Mario Martinez at Los Angeles, USA
19 April 1985	W KO6	Ruben Castillo at Inglewood, USA
7 July 1985	W KO2	Roger Mayweather at Las Vegas, USA
21 September 1985	W Pts12	Dwight Pratchett at Las Vegas, USA
15 May 1986	W KO5	Faustino Barrios at Paris, France
13 June 1986	W KO7	Refugio Rojas at New York, USA
3 August 1986	W Pts12	Rocky Lockridge at Monte Carlo, Monaco
12 December 1986	W Pts12	Juan LaPorte at New York, USA
18 April 1987	W KO3	Francisco Tomas Da Cruz at Nimes, France
21 August 1987	W Pts12	Danilo Cabrera at Tijuana, Mexico

WBA lightweight		
21 November 1987	W TKO11	Edwin Rosario at Las Vegas, USA
16 April 1988	W TKO6	Rodolfo Aguilar at Las Vegas, USA

WBC and WBA lightweight		
29 October 1988	W Pts11	Jose Luis Ramirez at Las Vegas, USA

WBC junior-welterweight		
13 May 1989	W TKO10	Roger Mayweather at Inglewood, USA
16 December 1989	W TKO3	Alberto Cortez at Mexico City, Mexico

WBC and IBF junior-welterweight		
8 December 1990	W KO3	Kyung Duk Ahn at Atlantic City, USA
18 March 1991	W KO4	Johnny Duplessis at Las Vegas, USA

WBC junior-welterweight		
14 September 1991	W Pts12	Lonnie Smith at Las Vegas, USA
10 April 1992	W TKO5	Angel Hernandez at Mexico City, Mexico
1 August 1992	W TKO4	Frank Mitchell at Las Vegas, USA
12 September 1992	W Pts12	Hector Camacho at Las Vegas, USA
20 February 1993	W TKO5	Greg Haugen at Mexico City, Mexico
8 May 1993	W TKO6	Terrence Alli at Las Vegas, USA

WBC welterweight		
10 September 1993	D Pts12	Pernell Whitaker at San Antonio, USA

WBC junior-welterweight		
18 December 1993	W KO5	Andy Holligan at Puebla, Mexico
29 January 1994	L Pts12	Frankie Randall at Las Vegas, USA
7 May 1994	W Pts8	Frankie Randall at Las Vegas, USA
17 September 1994	W TKO8	Meldrick Taylor at Las Vegas, USA
10 December 1994	W KO10	Tony Lopez at Monterrey, Mexico
8 April 1995	W Pts12	Giovanni Parisi at Las Vegas, USA

16 September 1995	W Pts12	David Kamau at Las Vegas, USA
7 June 1996	L TKO4	Oscar de la Hoya at Las Vegas, USA
7 March 1998	D Pts12	Miguel Angel Gonzalez at Mexico City, Mexico
WBC welterweight		
18 September 1998	L TKO8	Oscar de la Hoya at Las Vegas, USA

LITTLE BIG MAN

Kostya will be reduced to a pussycat.
He'll purr like a pussycat.
— flamboyant promoter Don King

The next step in my quest to unify the world titles would be made in Las Vegas a fraction over two years after I had won the first of the 'big three', the WBC crown. On 3 February 2001, I would go in against American southpaw Sharmba Mitchell, who held the WBA version of the world championship. Mitchell was big on hype. He would always describe himself as 'a warrior', cashing in on the fact that he was an African-American named after the legendary king of an African warrior tribe. At other times his publicity people called him 'Little Big Man'. He certainly had a big mouth. That's the way American boxing promoters liked their fighters. After all, talk is cheap.

I was taking no chances. I brought out to Australia two handy sparring partners from the United States. There was Corey Johnson, the challenger I had beaten in Sydney four-and-a-half years earlier. He had built up to fight as a junior-middleweight, and that would give me some tough preparation in the ring. Another sparring partner was David Sample, a classy junior-welterweight with a record of 29 wins and a draw from his 37 bouts over the previous 12 years. He had gone 12 rounds with Miguel Angel Gonzalez and, in the past, great fighters such as Sugar Ray Leonard, Azumah Nelson and Oscar de la Hoya had sought him out to spar with them in the lead-up to world title fights. I needed Johnson because he fought in a similar style to Mitchell. My third sparring partner was Gairy St Clair, a fighter from Guyana, who had stayed on after the fight and settled in Australia. I sparred more than 150 rounds with the three of them as part of my solid preparation.

I knew that Mitchell wasn't taking me for granted either. He had hired a celebrity fitness and nutrition guru named Mackie Shilstone to help him reach his peak. He was known for his regular appearances on American television shows such as *Today* and *Good Morning America*. Shilstone boasted of being a consultant to major sporting teams such as the Minnesota Vikings, the San Francisco Giants and the Toronto Blue Jays. The guru had also achieved a lot of publicity from his efforts to help Hollywood stars Wesley Snipes and Mickey Rourke shed excess weight for their movie roles. Shilstone had taken time out from a promotional tour for his new book *Lose Your Love Handles* to help out my opponent. I didn't need such assistance. I was fighting fit, and I already had a nutritional regimen better than any other I had ever seen.

Mitchell had also engaged William Joppy, who had just regained the WBA world middleweight title he had first won four years earlier. I was pleased when Mitchell's manager explained the logic of sparring with a world champion from three divisions heavier:

'Sharmba wanted to get accustomed to being hit harder than a normal junior-welterweight. After all, Kostya Tszyu hits harder than any middleweight in the world.' I knew as soon as I heard these words that I already had Mitchell beaten mentally. I was even happier when my spies told me that Joppy was smashing Mitchell from one corner of the ring to another in their sparring sessions at the Neutral Corner Gym in New Orleans. This would undoubtedly further mentally scar my opponent. The owner of the gym was an expatriate Australian, John Carmody. He was none too impressed by Mitchell's showing: 'What I've seen in the two weeks since Mitchell arrived here tells me Tszyu will win in nine or 10 rounds. Mitchell is tailor-made for him.'

Nevertheless, Mitchell was boasting, 'I have far too many skills for Tszyu. I will blind Tszyu with science. He is far too slow to catch me. They talk about his punching power, but I can punch, too, as he will find out.' It made me laugh. Every time I came up against an opponent from the United States they would claim I was too slow, or sometimes too weak, or lacking in boxing skills.

I had studied Mitchell's fights on videotape and knew he would probably jab and quickly duck for cover. Jab, jab, jab until he thought he had seen an opening. I was not worried. I told journalists I had several plans, depending on what happened in the ring. Plans A, B, C and ultimately D. Plan A — if he was going to run, I knew what to do. Plan B — if he pressured me, I knew what to do. Plan C — if he stood in front of me in defiance, I knew what to do. Plan D — well that was top secret.

I flew out of Sydney two weeks before the fight. Johnny said he was very happy with my preparation. He reckoned there was a real sharpness to all my work, especially my jabs. Johnny went on record as saying, 'Kostya has taken Mitchell's putdown that he lacks speed as an insult. He will make the American pay.' That wasn't quite right. I wasn't insulted. I just knew that by talking that way, Mitchell was worried.

Corey Johnson's summation of our sparring sessions would have had Mitchell even more worried: 'Kostya will chop him down with body shots and win by a knockout in the late rounds. He's punching harder than when we fought for the title, and that's truly frightening. He's become even more ring-wise. I regularly tried to outfox him, but he had read my moves almost before I thought of them.'

One of the newspapers had quoted Johnny as saying a disaster in Las Vegas would bring about the end of my career. That surprised me, as everyone in our camp was so confident that there was no thought of disaster at all. I believed in my ability. I believed in all the good preparation I had done. I believed in myself. When another reporter questioned me about Johnny's alleged comment I just laughed and suggested I would have to give Johnny a few jabs to sort it all out.

Once firmly established at the Mandalay Bay Hotel in Las Vegas, I continued my solid workouts. A week before the bout I had one of my best sparring sessions of the campaign with David Sample. The media were shut out, but Johnny made sure they knew about it, letting slip that in four rounds Sample hadn't been able to lay a glove on me.

Mitchell had a fine record. He had begun his professional career around the time I was fighting at the Seoul Olympics. He had lost just two of his 49 bouts. Incredibly they were back-to-back fights seven years earlier. One of his conquerors was a more-than-useful lightweight called Levander Johnson, the other a future WBC world lightweight champion, Stevie 'Lil But Bad' Johnston. Mitchell had held a number of minor titles, including the North American Boxing Federation lightweight championship, the WBC Continental Americas light-welterweight crown and the WBA Latin America junior-welterweight championship, before winning his version of the world title in October 1998. He had never been noted for knockout punches, with his four title defences all being won on points.

Mitchell's boasting continued as fight night approached:

> I rate myself up there with the best boxers of all time. Up there with Sugar Ray Leonard, Muhammad Ali and Roy Jones. I have taken my style from a lot of places. A little bit of Ali. Some Hector Camacho. I try to do a little Sugar Ray Robinson. I have the heart of Leonard and his will to win. I feel like Muhammad Ali before the famous [1974 heavyweight title fight] 'Rumble in the Jungle' with George Foreman. I will prevail with my boxing skills. Kostya will not be able to adapt. He punches real good and he likes to press. If you stand in front of him he can do it well. If you're not there to take the punches, how well can he do? We'll see when I get in the ring with him. Mark my words — I'll outbox him. It's not my southpaw style that will worry him. It's me — period. The way I fight will worry the death out him.

The fast-talking promoter Don King, whose son Carl was also Mitchell's co-manager, would not be outdone by his fighter:

> I've had nightmares when I've lain down to sleep. In the silence of the night, when nobody's there but me and my Maker, I see this devastating machine from Down Under demolishing my man Sharmba, but then suddenly I have this vision of David with five stones and a slingshot, and he fells the terrifying Goliath. Kostya is a Goliath. Thunder everywhere he walks. Thunder from Down Under, and cumulus clouds bouncing up and down, but we have found the secret to defuse this bomb. Sharmba Mitchell is David. He will give him a boxing lesson. Kostya will be reduced to a pussycat. He'll purr like a pussycat.

Yes. Purring like a pussycat lapping up milk. As for Mitchell's claims to have a bit of half a dozen of the all-time great boxers in his repertoire, he had to be kidding himself.

The disgraced heavyweight Mike Tyson was planning to be at the fight. He had persuaded Don King to give him five ringside tickets for himself and his flunkies. Before the fight, Tyson was shouting my praises, but I knew what his presence was all about. His management was involved with IBF champion Zab Judah, and when I beat Mitchell, the next step in the unification process was a fight with Judah.

'Mitchell is a slick boxer,' Tyson told a group of journalists and interested bystanders at the hotel. 'He will jab and run, but Kostya will stalk him and destroy him. He will have too much power in his fists. It will be a different matter in his next fight. He won't beat my boy, Zab Judah.' As it turned out Tyson did not turn up at the fight. If he had, he would have had to revise his opinion.

Back in Australia, certain sections of the media were worrying about the link between King and the referee, Joe Cortez. This pair had been at the centre of the contentious drawn world title bout in Las Vegas a decade earlier, when Jeff Fenech outboxed the champion Azumah Nelson but failed to get the verdict. Cortez had also been the referee at the centre of controversy in my 1997 bout with Puerto Rican Leonardo Mas. The newspapers and electronic media back home were offering suggestions that I would be ripped off if the Mitchell fight went the distance. The *Sun-Herald* reported Johnny's fears:

The memory of the Fenech-Nelson draw never fades. So, I suppose, you can't help thinking about the possibility of that sort of thing happening again, but the obvious answer is to make sure the result is taken out of the hands of the judges by ending it early. When you aim for a knockout you can put your fighter off his rhythm. Our goal is to win the fight — no matter how long it takes to achieve this aim. If there is a chance to end it early, Kostya will take it.

The journos back in Sydney tried to get Fenech to add his voice to the 'panic' story, but Jeff wouldn't play ball. He told the *Sun-Herald* among others:

You know I don't like that referee, and I know exactly what can happen when you have to rely on judges for a fair result, but I was in a completely different situation to Kostya when I went to America to fight Nelson. It was my first time in the country. I was unknown in the United States. I had some great victories under my belt, but I was a nobody to the powers-that-be over there, but Kostya is a big name in boxing — a big name in the United States. He's too big for it to happen to him. Anyway, there won't be a points decision. Kostya's far too good for this bloke. Mitchell will be leaving in a hearse.

I didn't like Jeff's choice of words. You never joke about death in the ring, but I was not worried about Don King. I was not worried about Joe Cortez, and I wasn't really worried about Sharmba Mitchell. I knew I had his measure.

On the day of the weigh-in, WBC president Jose Sulaiman announced I had been voted one of the 10 greatest boxers of the 1990s. It was an honour to be in the company of such names as Lennox Lewis, Roy Jones Jnr, Julio Cesar Chavez and Oscar de la Hoya. It was a real morale booster on a week in which King and Mitchell had hogged the headlines with their public utterances.

The gamesmanship continued right up until the fight. Mitchell demanded a guarantee of certain money allegedly owed to him before he would step onto the scales at the weigh-in. Then when he arrived in his dressing room, he sent word to me that the fight would have to be postponed because he was ill. That didn't work and half-an-hour later he sent another message. An old knee injury was playing up and he would not be able to fight properly.

'Stiff cheddar,' I replied using a typical Australian quip. I was there to fight, and fight I would. All this nonsense would have eroded Mitchell's mental preparedness. He was just playing into my hands.

The American certainly didn't have any knee problem when the fight started. In the first few rounds he was running like a rabbit. When he wasn't running he was trying to clinch, with his head bobbing around dangerously. I had to keep throwing him away in case a headbutt opened a cut on my face, and when I tossed him out of the way, one of his elbows used to come perilously close to my face. Referee Cortez did me no favours, allowing Mitchell's delaying tactics and docking a point from my score in the fourth round for pushing the American to the canvas.

As the fight progressed I was catching him more and more times with heavy blows. One of my left hooks opened a deep gash over his right eye. Another split open his bottom lip. He was not a pretty sight as I ripped into him in the sixth and seventh rounds. In the seventh he went down for the fifth time and allegedly twisted a leg as he hit the canvas. Whether or not he did so, I'll never know, but that was the excuse his team gave for throwing in the towel before the start of the eighth round. Mitchell was bloodied and beaten. He could not walk unaided, being propped up by two of his entourage as he staggered to his dressing room and then to hospital.

The victory had been decisive, but I wasn't really satisfied with my effort. It wouldn't have been a good fight to watch. There was too much clinching by Mitchell. My accuracy was not there and my punches weren't as sharp as they should have been, and I allowed too many of Mitchell's punches to get through my defences – even though they weren't telling punches. Whether or not the gap of seven months between fights was to blame I'm not sure, but I would have to work on it all before my next fight. Judah was ringside and immediately began mouthing off:

> I'm not impressed. He got hit a lot and was very slow with his jabs. With my quickness and power, I'll take his titles. Kostya is a good fighter who fought a smart fight, but that will not be enough against me. He goes straight forward with no special effects. When I put on my effects, I'll be in 3D and it will be all over. I'll take him apart, punch holes in him like a piece of Swiss cheese. Sharmba fought the wrong fight. You don't fight a bull by going backwards. You've got to go side to side with lateral movement. You've got to use your head, use your jabs and stick your uppercuts and hooks into him. Sharmba didn't do that. Tszyu will be no match for me. When I'm in trouble I turn into Superman. I put that kick on. I just transform. Believe me, my jabs are going to be pumping.

Zab had forgotten about kryptonite. If he saw himself as Superman, I saw myself as having kryptonite in my gloves.

SHARMBA MITCHELL (USA)		
World title fights		
WBA junior-welterweight		
10 October 1998	W TKO10	Khalid Rahilou at Paris, France
6 February 1999	W Pts12	Pedro Saiz at Washington, USA
24 April 1999	W Pts12	Reggie Green at Washington, USA
13 November 1999	W Pts12	Elio Ortiz at Las Vegas, USA
16 September 2000	W Pts12	Felix Flores at Las Vegas, USA

Other title fights		
North American lightweight		
6 November 1993	W TKO1	Chad Broussard at Las Vegas, USA
18 March 1994	L KO8	Levander Johnson at Las Vegas, USA
WBC Continental Americas junior-welterweight		
11 April 1996	W KO2	Gilberto Flores at Dallas, USA
WBA Latin American junior-welterweight		
10 May 1997	W Pts12	Jose Barboza at Miami, USA

In preparation for the Judah fight I went back to Uncasville to take on the Istanbul-born German Oktay Urkal on 23 June 2001. It was a mandatory defence of my title against the No. 1 contender for my WBC crown.

There was no way I would underestimate the challenger, as he was unbeaten in 28 fights as a professional. It was significant that all his fights except three had been on his home turf, in Germany. He'd fought a bloke in Switzerland early in his career and had a bout with British welterweight Karl Taylor in Norwich, England, in 1988. His only fight in the United States was a six-rounds points victory over a very ordinary Mexican fighter, Oscar Gabriel Gonzalez, at the Orleans Casino in Las Vegas 18 months before Urkal and I squared up.

I reckoned I should be able to overcome him, as he came from a typical European amateur background with which I was familiar. He had more than 200 fights as an amateur, the highlight being a silver medal at the 1996 Atlanta Olympics. He had lost on points in Atlanta to a great Cuban, Hector Vincent Charon, the reigning Olympic champion and the winner of the previous two world amateur titles. I knew from watching videos of Urkal's bouts he had a fast right hand and a deadly left. I would also have to overcome his height and reach. At 1.75 metres, he was seven centimetres taller than I was. But for nearly all my career I had to contend with this disadvantage.

In the lead-up to the fight I had perfected a new right-hand punch. It is very difficult to describe, but involves the way the right wrist is positioned when making contact. I told the Aussie media covering the fight that when I hit the bag with my new punch I could feel the bag tremble. Johnny told them that when I used it in the ring I had left a sparring partner with a very sore ear.

'The punch just adds another dimension to what Kostya has accumulated in his repertoire over his years in the sport,' Johnny added with a knowing smile.

It was an intriguing night of boxing in Uncasville. One of those on the undercard was Vince Phillips, the bloke who had taken my IBF title off me, and in the main preliminary bout was the current holder of that title, the loud-mouthed Zab Judah. He was defending it against Denmark's Allan Vester (who had an impressive 18 victories and one draw in his 19 career appearances).

Judah had conducted a one-man propaganda campaign against me in the week leading up to our respective title defences, dismissing me as a 'nothing' boxer. Journalists kept asking me about Judah. I told them I couldn't care less about Judah. I had the fight against Urkal to think about. I had to destroy him, and when I did, then maybe, just maybe, I would think about Judah. Anyway, he had to beat Vester to have any credibility, I told the journalists.

He did, knocking out the Dane in the third round of their bout. He had knocked him down twice in Round Two before grounding him again with a right hook near the end of the next round. This time Vester couldn't get back to his feet. Judah was cruel in his summation of the fight: 'When I hurt a guy I'm used to finishing him off. He kicked around in the second, but in the next round I put him out of his misery.'

Then Judah sat at ringside to watch my bout and, I am told, he mocked my efforts. I never heard him, but apparently Judah spent the whole fight taunting me, shouting out insults.

Right from the moment I arrived in Uncasville, the promoters made it crystal clear that they would like to have me beaten. The Americans didn't want me to be the champion because at 31 I was getting too old for their liking. They would have preferred a younger champion (and one that would shoot off at the mouth when the television cameras were rolling).

I couldn't believe how I was kept waiting for almost four hours to record a pre-fight television interview. Then there was the farcical weigh-in. First of all, it went on and on and on. Then they claimed I was a pound (2.2 kilograms) over the limit. This was bulldust. At first, they didn't want to let me check my weight the day before the official weigh-in. When they did I found the reading on their massive, old-style scales matched exactly the figure on the personal computerised scales on which I weigh myself every night and every morning of my life. Just before the official weigh-in I checked the weight on my scales and I was exactly on the 140 pounds (63.5 kilograms) limit, but, lo and behold, when I stepped on their scales I was a pound overweight and had to go away and sweat off the weight. Someone obviously tampered with the scales. Why in this computer age do they still use antiquated old scales? They claim it looks more spectacular on television. I say it's very suspicious.

When I finally got in the ring, I found a vocal group of about 20 hecklers sitting adjacent to my corner. They shouted abuse all through the fight and even after it.

I was right not to underestimate Urkal. He was a very tough competitor and took me the full distance. It was the first time I had been taken to 12 rounds since the Newcastle bout against Roger Mayweather six years earlier.

Urkal was a willing opponent, swapping blow for blow from the opening round. I kept working on him with my right ... jab, jab, jab ... to run up a good points lead in the early rounds. Urkal came back in the fifth and the sixth with some quick combinations.

He often looked tired but dug deep when I hit him with some powerful body blows and some stinging uppercuts that would have shaken a lesser man. He eased off from the seventh round after one of my solid left uppercuts broke his jaw. He was a tough fellow. He didn't show any hint of the pain he must have felt from the fracture. In the last round he knew he was well behind on points and came at me with the ferocity of a tiger trying for a knockout that could end the match. I managed to fend off the best of his blows.

In the end I got the vote from all three judges, 115-113, 116-113 and 116-112. I was happy with the result. I felt it was good to be taken the distance by such a good fighter. With every fight I prepared for the possibility of 12 rounds, but usually I was able to destroy my opponent earlier. This time I had to show my skills as a boxer and call on all my inner resilience. The fact that Urkal had never been knocked off his feet in his professional career showed how tough he really was, and what about him carrying on with the broken jaw? I told the media that I had regarded the Urkal fight as my semi-final. 'Now it is time to bring on the final [against Judah],' I said. 'And I'm really looking forward to it.'

Johnny wasn't as pleased as I was with my effort, nor was he happy with the way a couple of the judges scored it as a very close contest. He told the media, 'I think Kostya will have to lift his game. We'll probably have to knock out Judah to ensure we get the decision. If Kostya leaves it in the hands of the judges, he's going to have an uphill battle.'

Judah quickly started shouting his own praises as well as downplaying my display. 'Tszyu is a one-dimensional fighter,' he sneered. 'He doesn't move his head. Soon I will be undisputed champion of the world with all three titles. I can't wait to show him who is the true champion.'

I just smiled. I was reminded of the 16th century proverb — 'Empty vessels make the most noise'.

OKTAY URKAL (Germany)		
World title fights		
WBC international light-welterweight		
17 January 1998	W TKO3	Craig Houk at Berlin, Germany
14 November 1998	W Pts12	Viktor Baranov at Munich, Germany
13 February 1999	W TKO2	Frederick Tripp at Stuttgart, Germany
10 July 1999	W Pts12	Pablo Sarmiento at Augsburg, Germany
19 February 2000	W Pts12	Mikhail Krivolapov at Berlin, Germany
Other title fights		
European light-welterweight		
19 February 2000	W Pts12	Mikhail Krivolapov at Berlin, Germany
7 October 2000	W Pts12	Gabriel Mapouka at Berlin, Germany

The day after I arrived home from Connecticut I picked up the *Daily Telegraph* and found that respected sporting columnist Mike Gibson was casting doubts over my ability to match it with Judah. It did not make for good reading:

> Bobby Czyz was the IBF light-heavyweight champion of the world. Never into waltzes, Bobby always turned up looking for a fight. Today he is a ringside TV commentator and a darned good one. Over the weekend, watching Kostya Tszyu labour to a points decision over challenger Oktay Urkal in defence of his WBA and WBC super-lightweight titles, Bobby observed: 'A fighter can grow old in a night.'

Czyz was referring to Tszyu, now 31, who suddenly looked every day of it as he struggled to withstand a finishing onslaught from a largely unknown slugger who refused to follow the script.

Boxing is a cruel sport. When fighters go, they go overnight. One minute they're lining up guys and knocking them out. The next, down they flop on the seat of their pants and they're never the same fighters again.

The eventual demise of a fighter is seldom a slow process. In the blink of an eye, years of punishment, hundreds of rounds of wear and tear in the ring and the gymnasium catch up. One night they're reaching for the stars. The next they're seeing them. It is often sad, it is never pretty.

They may not be knocked out. Like Tszyu, they may even battle their way to a points victory, but the telltale signs are there. They get hit more than they should. Their punches no longer carry the snap and power they used to. Their timing is shot.

In his win over Urkal, a tough Turkish-born son-of-a-gun based in Germany, Tszyu exhibited the signs of a boxer whose best days are featured in past issues of *Ring* magazine. Tszyu made heavy weather of an opponent he was expected to carve up. It was Tszyu who got hit. Far too often. At times, he just hung there like a dartboard on a pub wall, a standing target on legs that either wouldn't — or couldn't — carry him out of harm's way.

Tszyu struggled in a bout which ensured [Zab] Judah will start favourite when they climb into the ring for their $8 million superfight. In Tszyu's favour is that Judah has a tendency to get knocked down in fights. By the same token, he has a tendency to get back up again and knock you rotten.

Meanwhile [Johnny] Lewis has a lot of work to do with a champion who has been climbing into the ring since he was a kid.

Against Judah, in the most unforgiving sport of all, we will find out whether Tszyu can still stoke the boiler or whether he grew old on a night in Connecticut last weekend.

I wasn't angry about what Mike Gibson wrote. He is a newspaper columnist and that is his job. He has to write it as he sees it, and on this occasion he reckoned I had reached my use-by date. I knew otherwise. And so, one day, would Gibson. He was always very fair, unlike a lot of other journalists who I have on my personal black list, and if he were proved wrong he would always immediately apologise, and apologise in print. He was a true gentleman.

I had to keep explaining over and over again how I had been pleased with my performance against Urkal. He was definitely one of the toughest, if not the smartest, boxers I had ever fought against. There were others who were technically much, much better, but few of them were as tough. There was nothing wrong with my hands. There is never any problem when you punch brick veneer, but punching Urkal was like punching double brick.

The next fighter, Zab Judah, well, his chin was nowhere near as tough as Urkal's. And we all knew what happened to Urkal's chin.

34 WINNER TAKES ALL

Tszyu is like Swiss cheese to me — full of holes.
— Zab Judah

Zab Judah wanted our unification fight to take place in the casino in Uncasville where he had won four of his latest six bouts. It was like a hometown for the excitable American, being little more than a stone's throw from his native New York.

He had officially won his world crown there, beating Jan Piet Bergman, the former Commonwealth champion who had fallen victim to me four years earlier. Bergman had managed to knock him down. But Judah shook away the cobwebs and hit him with a flurry of punches that were so fast that slow motion was used in television replays to show their effectiveness as Judah knocked out the South African.

Judah's lone venture outside the United States was his worst. It was in Glasgow against the unbeaten Englishman Junior Witter, whose tactics caused Judah all sorts of problems. He ducked and weaved out of range of the American's punches. It was the first time in two years that the kid from the slums of Brooklyn had been taken the distance.

Needless to say, Vlad, who had won the right to promote the bout was not interested in using the Uncasville casino. He had been forced to use an American referee and two hometown judges. He was adamant about the venue and got his way. He decided on the MGM Grand Casino in Las Vegas, the arena at which I had won my first crown (when I beat Jake Rodriguez). Johnny Lewis was probably even more delighted than I was. 'The MGM Grand was where Kostya won his first world title,' he told journalists, with a broad smile creasing his face. 'Hopefully we can win this one just as convincingly.'

Zab Judah was furious about the fact that the fight had been taken away from his home territory where his management and the battalion of Zab hip-hop fans would have made life particularly difficult for us. He vented his spleen on Vlad.

'We had to give him everything,' Judah complained to American journalists. 'If we hadn't have given in we wouldn't have had the fight. I told Vlad Warton this is going to be your biggest fight, and it's going to be your last fight. I'm going to take your meal ticket away from you.'

What is it they say about 'he who laughs last ...'?

For a while it looked as if the events of September 11 might force a cancellation of the fight which was to be held on 2 November 2001. Johnny expressed his worries publicly: 'Something in the back of your mind tells you the fight might not happen because of the worldwide trouble. But that's all out of our control. We just keep our fingers crossed, and once we are there [in Las Vegas] we'll put it right out of our mind.' As far as I was concerned, I had shut out any thoughts of the awful tragedy of September 11. I couldn't be worrying about whether terrorists would strike again, and I wanted to show that sport was above all that.

Despite what all the so-called experts reckoned about the Urkal fight, I was glad it had gone the way it had. One of the good things to come out of that fight was that I didn't rush. I didn't try to go in at 100 miles an hour trying to finish him off. That way you lay yourself open to a lucky punch that could knock you out. I kept my cool, knew what I was doing and kept saying to myself, 'If this goes the distance, don't be disappointed, be pleased'.

Sometimes you need long, tough fights to boost your own confidence. It's a comfortable feeling to know you can go the distance without any problem. I was not worried about either my mental or physical preparation for the unification bout. However, there were other problems that had to be addressed.

Security was one. I had my own team looking after me. Food was another. I told the Aussie journalists that I would step up my security, especially that in the kitchen of the hotel. Was I paranoid? After all, you don't hear of boxers being poisoned. But I had read of cases of top sportsmen and women becoming ill under suspicious circumstance on the day of a big event. I wasn't pointing the finger at Judah. He was all talk and wouldn't do such a thing. But maybe someone else? I just wasn't taking any chances. What I didn't tell anyone was that Papa had decided that when we ate a meal, sometimes he would eat the one prepared for me, and I would eat his. He was acting as a human guinea pig, like the food tasters of the Roman Emperors.

He's finished. He's made for me like a three-piece suit. I just gotta go to the tailor and get the right fit. He's weak mentally. He walks straight in and doesn't move his head after he punches. That's a bad habit. A good boxer with a good skill like mine will break him down. Urkal didn't have the power to finish him off, but what's he gonna do when a guy with my speed and power hits him?

We've been ringside at Tszyu's latest two fights and we were not impressed. As soon as he gets hit with a good punch, he will go back to the same old Kostya Tszyu that lost his world title. He is not a good enough fighter to be able to switch his whole style up the middle of a fight when he needs to. He is unable to do something else. He's a very one-dimensional fighter. He is very hittable. Tszyu is like Swiss cheese to me — full of holes.

Judging by his last fight, against Urkal, age is setting in. He's at the end of his career. He has only a couple of options against me — to come forward, try to pressure me, to throw the right hand, swing a hook and try to get in a lucky punch. It's only a lucky punch that will hit me.

Kostya's style is to walk up to you, straightforward, hoping you will stand in front of him. Then he hopes to knock you out. Yeah, he's done well with that style in the past, but he's not a man who can stand on his tippy-toes and move around. He's too old. He can't pop you with a good jab, get in and out and slip a punch, but that's what I'm planning to do to him.

This is all about boxing. People all too often forget it is a science. Throughout the years it has been proven over and over again that a super boxer, like me, can beat a puncher, like Tszyu, any day. Comparing Kostya with me is like comparing a Toyota four-wheel drive with a Mercedes.

Muhammad Ali is known as the greatest ever but not because of his power. Ali was the greatest because of his boxing ability. I'm here to box and show lots of speed and lateral movement. I will out-manoeuvre Tszyu. It will be like the bull and the matador. Ole!

I do give Tsyzu credit for one thing. He's 31 and still manages to get up for these kind of fights.

But everything is falling into place beautifully for me. I've just had a birthday and I've got a new baby, a beautiful girl called Destiny.

Destiny … my destiny is in the ring with Tszyu. It's time for me to unify the title.

It will be the end of Tszyu. He will be finished. As the posters say — 'Winner takes all'. I'm taking it all and there will be no second chance for Tszyu. He will have to go home and get another job. Winner takes all!

Oh boy, was Zab a real motormouth, or what? Trash-talking at its best — or should I say worst.

If it wasn't Judah mouthing off, it was one of his entourage. His manager was Shelly Finkel, an entrepreneur who once staged rock concerts for such superstars as Bob Dylan and The Grateful Dead. He had manoeuvred his way into the boxing game and regularly made headlines as an adviser/manager to Mike Tyson. He was now Judah's manager and was talking him up: 'I was watching Zab in training, away from all the hype, and he's the best I've ever seen him. He's faster and punching harder than he has ever done. He is most certainly a better fighter than he was a year ago. There's no doubt about that.'

In an ironic twist, Judah had come off second best in a confrontation with hoodlums in a Brooklyn street a few months earlier. These people were no respecters of his trash-talk. He had been driving a flash car through the slum, flaunting his riches (he was said to be wearing around a quarter of a million dollars worth of jewellery at the time). He made the mistake of stopping the car and a bloke shoved a gun in his face. They got away with jewellery and a watch and plenty of cash. Judah explained at one of his many press conferences: 'I came around with this drop-top Prowler, jewellery and they're standing there going: "Man, I ain't ate in a week and you're going to come around here with all that!" It was a humbling experience for me.'

Humbling? He didn't sound too humble to me.

Unfortunately boxing and showbiz are very close to each other. I suppose that's because boxing is a form of entertainment. American promoters loved the hip-hop jive talk of Zab, especially when he flashed a smile and revealed his four sparkling gold teeth, but to me that was too much like professional wrestling, which no one in their right mind takes seriously.

Robert Lusetich, the Los Angeles correspondent for News Limited who had come to Las Vegas for the fight, summed it succinctly as he described a media gathering:

As is his way, Kostya Tszyu sat quietly on the podium at the MGM Grand Casino yesterday, tuning out the clichéd histrionics which are the equivalent of ringside spit buckets at pre-fight news conferences — serving a purpose but repugnant to gaze upon. After removing his blue-tinged sunglasses, he made clear his disdain of everything about boxing that's not about boxing.

As I told that conference, I didn't need hype. I left that to Judah, and it didn't worry me that all his big-mouthing had made him a favourite with the Las Vegas bookmakers and left me the 3-1 outsider. I knew that all the hype was a smokescreen for something else — fear. He was rating himself much too highly. His team was doing the same, but through all that supposed confidence I could smell the fear.

Judah was insecure, wild and unpredictable. He was a good thinker, had great speed and real physical power in both hands. But he had been put down on his backside by three of those he had fought while defending his world crown — Bergman, Reggie Green and Terronn Millett. Judah was young. Indeed, he was the youngest world champion I had ever encountered in the ring. I had fought a host of champs before him, but they were experienced and fought with incredible cunning. Judah had never experienced certain things in the ring. He had never been in tough fights. He had never been in situations where his body had lost it and he didn't know what to do. That is a place of extra desire. That is where you have to dig deep into that source of inner strength. I had been there and experienced that physical and mental trauma. I knew where to look for that inner strength.

People pointed to my age, as if that was a disadvantage, but, to me, my age was a distinct advantage. The way I looked at it was that Judah hadn't fought blokes of the calibre that I had beaten. That's what is simply called experience. I may have been 31, but I had yet to reach my peak. My experience told me I would need to have plenty of options to foil Judah's tactics that would rely on speed. I had worked on two styles of jab — the sharp, snappy jab and the heavy, powerful one. Different combinations to bamboozle him in what I believed was going to be a very tactical fight, a hard fight, a fight we would remember for many, many years.

People kept asking me: Would it be a knockout? Or would I have to settle for a win on points? I would tell them over and over again. It makes no difference to me. When and how victory comes, it comes and everyone will see.

I knew I had the winning trifecta — my mind, my power, my experience.

It will be such a great fight because they are so completely different. One is young, the other old. One depends on his speed, the other on his power. It will be a torrid battle, with the winner being the one with the best options on the night. The key to success will be Kostya's jab. A good, hard, quick jab can open the way for the heavy artillery to come into play. Judah has the speed around the ring. He moves with lightning speed and he throws good combinations of punches. Kostya must use his jab to counter that speed and set Judah up for the big punches.

His preparation for the fight has been spot-on, something that I couldn't say about the fights with Mitchell and Urkal. On both occasions I reckoned he had peaked back home in Australia a few weeks before the fights. This time he looks a treat and is ready to peak in the ring.

Kostya has to fight Judah, not box him. There's a subtle difference. He's got to take Zab into a realm where he has never been before, a realm where he will be out of his depth both mentally and physically.

Kostya's advantage is what I describe as his 'ring savvy'. As a boxer he has got it all. He is the complete fighter. High skill levels. Heavy punching power, and, above all, dogged determination. It was this determination that helped drag him up from the depths of despair after the Phillips defeat. It is the determination that will prove the difference when he steps into the ring with Judah. Zab is very dangerous, but I still wouldn't swap Kostya for anyone.
— *Johnny Lewis*

I was feeling good, but more so when I listened to what Johnny was telling others. He was so confident and that buoyed my own confidence. I also knew I had the whole of Australia behind me. I was getting about 300 emails a day on my website, and reading through these messages of support helped lift me, too. I knew I could not let down all these people. It was going to be an important fight for me, for my family, for my team (Team Tszyu) and for my fans (Tszyu Crew).

I was intrigued by how other people saw my chances. Intrigued but not worried by what they said. After all, I knew my fate would be decided by me and me alone.

• Angelo Dundee, the famed boxing trainer who guided the great Muhammad Ali to his world heavyweight titles: 'Kostya will win by a knockout.'

- Roy Jones Jnr, arguably the finest boxer of the past quarter of a century: 'Judah's going to have trouble taking Kostya's punch.'

- Vince Phillips, the only bloke ever to beat me: 'Tszyu will beat Judah easily. Tszyu is really strong. Although I stopped him, he's the toughest guy I ever fought.'

- The respected *The Ring* magazine: 'Kostya will have to improve on his last two fights if he is to win.'

- That infamous heavyweight embarrassment to boxing, Mike Tyson: 'My boy Zab will cream the Russian.'

- Jeff Fenech responded with: 'Mike Tyson assured me his boy would win. I knew otherwise. I bet on Kostya to win by a knockout in the first three rounds. At odds of 25-1, I stood to win a lot of money, but I reckoned it was a safe bet.'

- American welterweight Dave Sample, one of my sparring partners during the preparation for the fight: 'I don't think the fight will go past eight rounds. Zab fights a lot with his chin in the air. Kostya will catch him.'

- Noted American boxing journalist Frank Gonzalez: 'The bout will go the distance, with Zab winning a questionable decision.'

Judah seemed relatively subdued in the ring before the bout. After the weigh-in I was convinced I had him psyched. Seeing him in the ring waiting while all the official announcements were made only convinced me more. The cockiness was no longer there, and his eyes, I saw it in his eyes, they were the eyes of a beaten man, not the eyes of a champion. I am told that Tyson was next to him in the parade from the dressing room, whispering in his ear all the way to the ring. I wonder what he said to Zab. Whatever it was it didn't help dispel the obvious fear that lurked inside my opponent.

But it was typical Judah as the fight began. He bounced into the centre of the ring and immediately began throwing a flurry of quick punches. Zip, zip, zip they came. He was certainly fast, but most of the punches were missing. I'm told the ringside television commentators were in raptures, but they didn't see how I evaded most of them. Halfway through the round he whipped in with a wonderful left uppercut. It caught me a glancing blow and I backpedalled as he tried to follow up the advantage. It was the overconfidence of youth. He thought he had me and it was only a matter of time before he could finish me off. How cruel this world can be. Late in the round I caught him with a heavy punch to the liver and another to the head. The liver punch certainly slowed him a lot.

In Round Two I began stalking my prey. He didn't realise it, but I was steering him around the ring in preparation for a couple of monster blows. He was flashy, still darting around with exaggerated movements, waving his arms and twisting his head. It might have looked good on television. It certainly looked good to me. No matter which way he went I was already there, ready to cut him off. My time was fast approaching. It was near the end of the round. I quickly stopped his histrionics. I feinted and he fell for it, hook, line and sinker. I caught him in the neck with a left jab and, as his body rolled with the punch, I crashed a right into his head, then a second hard right and he went spinning to the canvas. His head hit the canvas with a sickening thud. Judah was as good as out, but inexplicably he staggered back to his feet.

I glanced at the referee, Jay Nady, to see if he was going to stop the fight. For a moment I thought he was going to let it continue, but Judah's legs weren't up to it. He weaved across the ring like a drunk at hotel closing time, legs splayed at right angles and arms swinging loosely at his side. Judah could have been back in Brooklyn for all he knew. As Nady waved the bout over, Judah fell down flat on his face. There was just one second left in the round.

I was over the moon. I had unified the world title. At last, after

33 years, there was just one world champion in my division. Only two others, Roy Jones (light-heavyweight) and Bernard Hopkins (middleweight), had previously unified their titles.

I had little time in the ring to celebrate. Judah had cleared his head and was livid when he realised he had lost. He threw a stool in the direction of Nady. Then his father-cum-trainer, Yo'el, and others from his corner jumped into the ring and surrounded the referee, screaming abuse at him. Suddenly Judah shoved his fist into Nady's throat and had to be manhandled away from him by security men. The uproar continued for several minutes and it took some police to break it up. As American journalist Frank Gonzalez described it, Judah was finally escorted out of the ring after kicking, screaming and crying like a spoiled baby who couldn't have his way.'

Meanwhile, with the three world championship belts draped over my shoulders, I was being interviewed by Showtime Television Network's Tim Smith:

Was Judah's speed a factor in this fight?

No. It wasn't an issue. I know I lost the first round, he hit me with some good shots. I was not impressed with his punching power, though. When I knocked him out, it wasn't even a very hard punch, just a well-timed blow. I am happy to have unified the title. This was my destiny. I trained for hours and hours for this fight. Now I have unified the super-lightweight championship. I am very happy to have won this way against a great opponent.

Does he deserve a rematch?

Do you remember the press conference, where he was asked the same question? He answered that the 'Winner takes all!' Now I answer the same way. It's not like a boomerang.

Someone else asked a question — I can't remember who it was —

and I told him why I knew I would win. I believed this was my destiny. I knew I had power in both hands. Both of them could knock out an elephant.

I think that this victory was my finest moment in boxing. As I explained at the time, my finest moment, not my final moment. It was a page in history. My kids and my grandkids would remember that day. It was the reason why I trained so hard, why I sweated every day, why pain was as normal as the sun rising in the east and setting in the west.

Judah's management was now crying foul. His manager Gary Shaw claimed Nady should have given a 10 count. He said he had immediately instructed his lawyers to start legal proceedings. 'It was incompetence on the part of the referee for not following the rules of the Nevada [Athletic] Commission and allow Zab to fight the next round,' he claimed. 'We will protest to the WBC, IBF and WBA.' Judah asked journalists, 'Why did he stop the fight? He didn't even give me a count.'

Nady stopped the fight because Judah was hurt. Had it continued Judah could have suffered lasting brain damage, as Nady explained: 'The man was hurt. I had to protect the fighter. I was concerned he might get hurt after getting hit with a very powerful punch that appeared to render him momentarily unconscious.' WBC president Jose Sulaiman jumped to Nady's defence: 'Another blow could have caused "second concussion syndrome" which can be fatal. Fortunately the referee stopped the fight. We are very proud of Jay Nady and the way he handled the situation. It will be included in future training videos for WBC referees.'

There was an intriguing interview with Judah in his dressing room. Poor old Zab was obviously still confused and disorientated:

 I was pulling back, I bet you … I got hit by a good shot, I went down, maybe I got up too fast … yeah, I mean, you're hurt …

okay … I mean, okay, you know … I was wobbly … you know what I mean? It's what type of fight? I got up too fast, you know … they gotta give you some time to get up … this is not like some, you know, this is a world title fight … you know what I mean, I've seen fighters roll around on the floor … he just never gave me a chance. Okay, I'm on the floor … I can't be wobbly on the floor, cut it out, man, don't try to be smart … look, look, he didn't even start the count on me, look, look … I mean, I guess … I don't know what was going through the ref's mind … look, look, I'm back. Hey, I can't cry about it, know what I mean, all I can do is come back. I'm a young fighter. Kostya Tszyu is a legend, know what I mean?

A confused Judah rambled on like this for several minutes. Sanity later prevailed and Judah apologised to Nady over his assault on him. The authorities then slapped him on the wrist with a feather, fining him US$75000 and imposing a six-month ban on him fighting. So what? He had just earned millions and he wouldn't be fighting for about six months anyway.

I was buoyed by the reaction to my win in the US media. Frank Gonzalez summed it up wonderfully: 'I confess that it was a real treat for me to see poetic justice. I thought Tszyu fought smartly against a very overrated fighter who has been coddled by his managers, promoters and hype-makers. Like other mouthy fighters who build their resumes on easy or fixed opponents, once they get in the ring with a real legitimate fighter, they are exposed.'

David Moya, of the boxing website diamondgloves.com, wrote a stinging rebuttal of the beaten American: 'We have to tip our hats to Kostya Tszyu for performing like a champion and carrying himself like a gentleman. Judah's fan base won't grow due to his post-fight actions and he may have self-destructed his entire career. To bring some clarity to the situation: Zab Judah, you are the weakest link!'

The morning after the fight we were leaving Las Vegas to come home. As we walked through the foyer of our hotel I noticed the figure of Zab Judah. There were no journalists milling around this time. No television cameras and microphones to catch him spouting his hip-hop talk. There was no entourage of fawning sycophants. Just Zab Judah by himself. A lonely beaten man. Did I feel sorry for him? Maybe. I never hate an opponent. And he *is* a good fighter. He will be world champion again one day, but not while I am still fighting.

ZAB JUDAH (USA)		
World title fights		
IBF junior-welterweight		
16 January 1999	W KO4	Wilfredo Negron at Las Vegas, USA*
12 February 2000	W KO4	Jan Piet Bergman at Uncasville, USA
24 June 2000	W Pts12	Junior Witter at Glasgow, Scotland
5 August 2000	W KO4	Terronn Millett at Uncasville, USA
20 October 2000	W KO8	Hector Quiroz at Auburn Hills, USA
13 January 2001	W TKO10	Reggie Green at Uncasville, USA
23 June 2001	W KO3	Allan Vester at Uncasville, USA

* interim title

EPILOGUE

I thought the embarrassment at Las Vegas would have shut Zab Judah's mouth. I should have known better. It was only days before he regained his bravado and was at his bad-mouthing worst. He wanted a rematch.

I read what he said with amusement, 'Kostya can have 100 per cent of the purse,' Judah said. 'It doesn't matter to me, I just want to fight and I'll fight for nothing. It's not about money no more. I'll fight him in Australia, Iowa, in his backyard, wherever. In everybody's eyes, they don't look at Kostya as a legitimate, bona fide champion. I'm back in the gym already, I'm training and I'm getting ready. If Kostya doesn't fight me, I'll fight someone else and I'll show the world that Zab Judah is still the best fighter out there. Without a belt, I'm still the champion.'

Without a belt? I had three belts and that said it all. Yet, every few weeks Judah would continue his tiresome diatribe. Some people never learn!

In April I heard the news that I would receive yet another belt. The respected American magazine *The Ring*, which for the 80 years of its existence had been regarded by everyone in the game as boxing's bible, announced it had had enough of the proliferation of world titles. The magazine was going to award its own world title

belts. There were just four ways a boxer could achieve the honour
— beat *The Ring* world champion; unify the three major titles; as one
high-profile champion beating another; or by the top two
contenders in *The Ring* ratings fighting for a vacant title. I was one
of eight champions who were to be recognised by the magazine
(another was my former victim Vernon Forrest).

The magazine's editor, Nigel Collins, was none too
complimentary to those behind the existing titles, 'Through the
years, we've seen what the alphabet organisations have done to
boxing. They've attached themselves like leeches slowly sucking the
blood out. It's one of the biggest problems facing boxing, the
mainstream sports fan doesn't know who the champions are.'

Well, in my case they certainly did.

I went back to Las Vegas in May 2002 and at the Mandalay Bay
Casino fought off a challenge from Ben 'Wonder' Tackie from
Ghana. The bout went the full 12 rounds. He just refused to give up
no matter how many punches rained down on him. He was like a
goalkeeper catching punches with his head. For some reason the
referee wouldn't stop the fight even though Tackie was taking so
much punishment.

BEN TACKIE (Ghana)		
Title bouts		
IBF intercontinental lightweight		
7 July 1998	W TKO9	Louie Leija at San Antonio, USA
North American light-welterweight		
10 August 2001	W Pts12	Ray Oliviera at Ledyard, USA
25 January 2002	W TKO5	Teddy Reid at Rosemount, USA

I came home to be with Natasha as we await the birth of our third child, a daughter, who will have been born by the time this book is published. We are as excited as we were when awaiting the arrival of her two brothers. And Natasha is doubly busy settling us in to our new house in Sydney. As for boxing, I have another title defence on 19 January 2003 against Jesse James Leija at Colonial Stadium in Melbourne.

And what will I do when I finally call it a day? I won't be able to leave boxing altogether. I am already involved with the country's amateur fighters, having taken the 'A' team to Moscow for an Australia versus Russia tournament while the top boxers were in Manchester for the 2002 Commonwealth Games. I think I have a lot to offer these young kids coming through.

The Tszyu Boxing Academy will eventually have some world-class boxers. I want to look after them and other talented Aussies to ensure they get the opportunity to follow in my footsteps and not get ripped off by professional boxing officials and hangers-on. We have a wonderful pool of talent in Australia. These future boxers must be nurtured and encouraged.

Will I push Timophey and Nikita into boxing, just as my papa did with me? I certainly won't push them, but if they want to be boxers I will be there to show them how to succeed. I will be there to guide them to their destiny.

THE GREATEST?

After Kostya Tszyu unified the world titles several renowned Australian boxing personalities went on record to name him as one of the greatest in the history of the sport.

• Respected boxing writer Grantlee Kieza rated Tszyu No. 1 in a list of the greatest junior-welterweights of all time. Kieza named Tszyu in front of American Aaron Pryor (world champion from 1980 to 1985), No. 3: Puerto Rican Wilfred Benitez (1976); No. 4: Oscar de la Hoya (1996 to 1997); No. 5: Julio Cesar Chavez (1989 to 1995); No. 6: American Barney Ross (1933 to 1935); No. 7: Antonio Cervantes of Colombia (1972 to 1980); No. 8: Englisman Jack 'Kid' Berg (1930 to 1931); No. 9: Nicolino Loche of Argentina (1968 to 1972); No. 10: Italian Duilio Loi (1960 to 1962).

• Veteran trainer Jack Rennie, who guided Lionel Rose to a world bantamweight title said, 'I've seen all the greats since the 1940s — fighters such as Pryor, Chavez in his prime, and de la Hoya. Kostya would have beaten all of them. His anticipation of an opponent's moves is phenomenal and he always throwing fast, loaded punches.'

• IBF vice-president and top boxing official Ray Wheatley: 'Kostya is a class above any junior-welterweight I have ever seen. He beat Chavez when he was past his prime but even if they had both met at the top of their games, Kostya's strength and power would have prevailed. Kostya has the know-how to work out any style and the power punch to capitalise when he does.'

• Australia's former IBF world junior-welterweight champion Barry Michael: 'Kostya is undoubtedly the greatest fighter ever to represent Australia. He is a tremendous puncher, very strong and very smart.

He has the strongest mental discipline I've ever seen in an athlete.'

• Referee of several world title fights and former Australian bantamweight champion Billy Males: 'He's the best puncher I have ever seen. And he fights with an incredible tunnel vision that allows him to block out everything but the man in front of him.'

APPENDIX II

DRAMATIS PERSONAE

ALEKSANDR BANIN: A Soviet amateur fighter who I beat (in a unanimous points decision) in the final of the 1990 Goodwill Games in Seattle.

SUSIE BENNELL: A Sydney member of Team Tszyu who became my business manager in 2000, taking charge of most things including sponsorship, media relations, marketing and merchandising.

JAN PIET BERGMANN: The South African champion who challenged me for the IBF world crown at Newcastle on 14 September 1996. I won by knockout in the sixth round.

LIVINGSTONE BRAMBLE: A former WBA world lightweight champion, from the Caribbean nation of Saint Kitts and Nevis. I beat him on points in our 10-round bout at Newcastle on 23 August 1993.

JULIO CESAR CHAVEZ: An almost legendary Mexican fighter and winner of six world titles in four weight divisions. I became only the second fighter in history to knock him off his feet as I successfully defended my WBC title with a sixth-round TKO at Phoenix, Arizona, on 29 July 2000.

RAY CONNELLY: One of the Bill Mordey team involved in my early professional fights. As well as being a respected boxing critic, he was a renowned ring announcer known for his unique introductions that made full use of alliteration.

DANIEL CUSATO: An Argentine welterweight who fought me in

Melbourne on 11 September 1992. I won when the referee stopped the fight in the seventh round.

SCOTT CRAMNE: The Liberian-born Swedish amateur champion and silver medal winner at the 1988 Seoul Olympics. I beat him in a semi-final of the 1989 European Championships in Athens.

OSCAR DE LA HOYA: An American who won a gold medal at the 1992 Barcelona Olympics. After turning professional he won world titles at several weights. He had often been mentioned as a possible opponent for me.

SHELLY FINKEL: An American entrepreneur who switched from staging rock concerts to managing fighters. Among his stable were notorious heavyweight Mike Tyson and Zab Judah, the man I beat in 2001 to unify the world titles.

VERNON FORREST: An American amateur champion and later, in the professional ranks, the WBC world welterweight champion. I beat him in the final of the 1991 world (amateur) championships in Sydney.

SAMMY FUENTES: A Puerto Rican who briefly held the WBC light-welterweight world title in 1989. I beat him with a first-round knockout in a Melbourne bout on 13 November 1992.

JULIO GONZALEZ: A Cuban amateur champion who beat me in a 1988 international tournament in Leningrad leading up to the Seoul Olympics.

MIGUEL ANGEL GONZALEZ: The renowned Mexican boxer who was a former WBC lightweight champion. When I successfully defended my world title against him at Miami on 21 August 1999, he had lost only one of his 45 bouts — to the great Oscar de la Hoya.

CALVIN GROVE: An American veteran and former IBF world featherweight champion. I knocked him out in the first round of our fight in Newcastle on 5 April 1998 in my second comeback fight after losing my IBF world junior-welterweight crown.

ANGEL HERNADEZ: A Puerto Rican fighter I knocked out in seven rounds at Newcastle, on 2 May 1994.

JUAN HERNANDEZ: The Cuban amateur champion who beat me in the 1987 World Junior Championships, a hometown decision in Havana.

DARRELL HILES: A Queenslander who fought me in my first professional fight, in Melbourne, on 1 March 1992. I won with a knockout in the first round.

DIOBELYS HURTADO: The Cuban exile who fell to me in five rounds at Indio, California, on 28 November 1998 for the vacant WBC junior-welterweight title.

COREY JOHNSON: A solid American who challenged me for the IBF world junior-welterweight title on 24 May 1996. I knocked him out in the fourth round.

TONY JONES: My third professional opponent. I knocked him out in the second round of our fight at Sydney, on 7 May 1992.

ZAB JUDAH: The flashy, trash-talking New Yorker who was IBF junior-welterweight champion of the world. I beat him in two rounds on 2 November 2001 to unify the three world titles.

LARRY LaCOURSIERE: An American fighter and the first opponent I fought in Newcastle. I knocked him out in the first round of our bout on 14 May 1993.

JUAN LaPORTE: A former WBC World Featherweight Champion. I beat him on points over 10 rounds in my fourth professional fight, at Sydney, on 23 July 1992.

STEVE LARRIMORE: A fighter from the Bahamas who had beaten Australian Lester Ellis to win the Commonwealth light-welterweight championship in 1989. I beat Larrimore in my first professional bout in the United States, at Memphis, Tennessee, on 30 January 1993. I won by a knockout in the second round.

JOHNNY LEWIS: My trainer during my professional career. He also trained Jeff Fenech and Jeff 'Hit Man' Harding while they were on a path to world championship status.

HECTOR LOPEZ: A tough Mexican who had fought unsuccessfully in 1993 for the WBC world lightweight championship. Nine months later, on 11 January 1994, I fought him in Tampa, Florida, in a bout in which I only just managed a points' victory.

LEONARDO MAS: A Puerto Rican boxer I knocked out in the first round of our Las Vegas bout on 18 January, 1997. But the referee declared the result a technical draw because he claimed I had hit Mas with a foul punch.

ROGER MAYWEATHER: An American they dubbed the Black Mamba. He had been WBA world super-featherweight champion in 1983 and WBC world light-welterweight champion from 1987 to 1989. I beat him on points over 12 rounds to retain my IBF world crown, at Newcastle on 25 June 1995.

TERRONN MILLETT: An American amateur star and later IBF world junior-welterweight champion. I beat him on a unanimous points decision in a semi-final at the 1990 Goodwill Games in Seattle.

BRIAN MILLS: A member of Bill Mordey's team, who became a dear friend while acting as our 'chauffeur' during our first months in Australia.

SHARMBA MITCHELL: The American holder of the WBA junior-welterweight crown threw in the towel after eight rounds when we fought at Las Vegas, on 3 February 2001, as I sought to unify the titles.

BILL MORDEY: A real character, with various nicknames including Blue Gum and Break Even Bill. He was an ex-journalist turned boxing promoter who persuaded me to fight professionally in Australia. We split amidst much acrimony after I won my first world title and a subsequent court case saw me forced to pay him around $4 million in damages.

HUGO PINEDA: The Latin American light-welterweight champion from Colombia. I knocked him out in the 11th round of our IBF title fight at Parramatta Stadium, on 20 January 1996.

ROBERT RIVERA: A Puerto Rican I knocked out in the first round of our bout in Newcastle, on 18 June 1993.

JAKE 'THE SNAKE' RODRIGUEZ: The Puerto Rican I beat to win my first world title, the IBF light-welterweight championship, at Las Vegas, on 28 January 1995. We became friends and he worked as my sparring partner later in my career.

RAFAEL RUELAS: The fine Mexican boxer I knocked out in the ninth round of a bout on 15 August 1998 in El Paso, Texas, as a prelude to my challenge for the WBC world title.

PEDRO SANCHEZ: A tough competitor from the Dominican Republic. They called him Toro Loco — the Mad Bull. I beat him in a fourth-round knockout at Melbourne, on 29 August 1994.

AHMED SANTOS: I beat this clever Mexican fighter with an eighth-round knockout at Uncasville, Connecticut, on 12 February 2000, to retain my WBC world crown.

NED SIMMONS: A Canadian fighter who lasted just one round in my second professional fight, in Sydney, on 2 April 1992.

BEN TACKIE: The African champion from Ghana who I beat at Las Vegas on 18 May 2002 in my first defence of the unified titles.

OKTAY URKAL: The Turkish-born German who gave me a tough fight when I defended my WBC and WBA crowns at Uncasville, Connecticut, on 23 June 2001. I took out a points decision over 12 rounds.

VLAD WARTON: The Russian-born Sydney businessman who became a close friend and, after the split with Bill Mordey, my manager and promoter.

ANDREAS ZUELOW: The East German amateur champion who won the gold medal at the 1988 Seoul Olympics. My record against Zuelow was four wins and two losses (at Seoul and in the 1989 World Championships in Moscow).

MY AMATEUR CAREER

270 bouts for 259 victories

World Championship:
Winner — 1991 in Sydney
Third — 1989 in Moscow

Goodwill Games:
Winner — 1990 in Seattle

European Championship:
Winner — 1989 in Athens *
& 1991 in Gothenburg
(Goeteborg)*

Soviet Championship:
Winner three times — 1989, 1990 and 1991
Second — 1988

World Junior Championship:
Second — 1987 in Havana

European Junior Championship:
Winner — 1986 in Brondby

Soviet Junior Championship:
Winner twice — 1986 and 1987

* Boxer of the Tournament

APPENDIX IV
MY PROFESSIONAL CAREER

1992

1 March	W KO1	Darrell Hiles at Melbourne, Australia
2 April	W KO1	Ned Simmons at Sydney, Australia
7 May	W TKO2	Tony Jones at Sydney, Australia
23 July	W Pts10	Juan LaPorte at Sydney, Australia
11 September	W TKO7	Daniel Cusato at Sydney, Australia
13 November	W TKO1	Sammy Fuentes at Melbourne, Australia

1993

30 January	W KO7	Steve Larrimore at Memphis, Tennessee, USA
14 May	W KO1	Larry LaCoursierre at Newcastle, Australia
18 June	W KO1	Robert Rivera at Newcastle, Australia
23 August	W Pts10	Livingstone Bramble at Newcastle, Australia

1994

11 January	W Pts10	Hector Lopez at Tampa, Florida, USA
2 May	W TKO7	Angel Hernandez at Newcastle, Australia
29 August	W TKO4	Pedro Sanchez at Melbourne, Australia

1995

28 January	W TKO6	Jake Rodriguez at Las Vegas, Nevada, USA
		(Won IBF junior-welterweight championship)
25 June	W Pts12	Roger Mayweather at Newcastle, Australia
		(Retained IBF junior-welterweight championship)

1996

20 January	W TKO11	Hugo Pineda at Sydney, Australia
		(Retained IBF junior-welterweight championship)
24 May	W KO4	Corey Johnson at Sydney, Australia
		(Retained IBF junior-welterweight championship)
14 September	W TKO6	Jan Bergman at Newcastle, Australia
		(Retained IBF junior-welterweight championship)

1997

18 January	TD1	Leonardo Mas at Las Vegas, Nevada, USA
		(Retained IBF junior-welterweight championship)
31 May	L TKO10	Vince Phillips at Atlantic City, New Jersey, USA
		(Lost IBF junior-welterweight championship)
6 December	W TKO3	Ismael Chaves at Townsville, Australia

1998

5 April	W TKO3	Calvin Grove at Newcastle, Australia
15 August	W TKO9	Rafael Ruelas at El Paso, Texas, USA
28 November	W TKO5	Diobelys Hurtado at Indio, California, USA
		(Won WBC super-lightweight championship*)

1999

21 August	W TKO10	Miguel Angel Gonzales at Miami, Florida, USA
		(Retained WBC super-lightweight championship)

2000

12 February	W TKO8	Ahmed Santos at Uncasville, Connecticut, USA
		(Retained WBC super-lightweight championship)
29 July	W TKO6	Julio Cesar Chavez at Phoenix, Arizona, USA
		(Retained WBC super-lightweight championship)

2001

3 February	W TKO7	Sharmba Mitchell at Las Vegas, Nevada, USA
		(Retained WBC super-lightweight championship)
		(Won WBA junior-welterweight championship)
23 June	W Pts12	Oktay Urkal at Uncasville, Connecticut, USA
		(Retained WBC & WBA championships)
2 November	W TKO2	Zab Judah at Las Vegas, Nevada, USA
		(Won IBF junior-welterweight championship)
		(Retained WBC & WBA championships) **

2002

| 18 May | W Pts12 | Ben Tackie at Las Vegas, Nevada, USA |
| | | (Retained WBC, WBA & IBF championships) |

* Interim title

** First boxer to unify all three titles in his division

BOXING TERMS

BOXING ORGANISATIONS

IBF — International Boxing Federation

IBO — International Boxing Organisation

WBA — World Boxing Association

WBC — World Boxing Council

WBO — World Boxing Organisation

FIGHT RESULTS

W — Win

L — Loss

D — Draw

TD — Technical draw (when one boxer can't continue after being disabled by an unintentional foul blow)

KO — Knockout (boxer counted out by the referee)

TKO — Technical knockout (referee stops the fight to prevent further injury to the beaten boxer)

Pts — Decision based on the votes of three judges sitting ringside